Praise Page

"*Field Stories*, edited by William Leggett and Ida Fadzillah Leggett, is a trenchant collection that focuses on the powerful force of the ethnographic field narrative. Anthropologists are avid storytellers, word weavers, emotion conjurers and co-world-makers. Ethnographic fieldwork is not about 'observing' life from afar, but is a series of engaged encounters, desires, attachments, and bonds. It is not a cold-hearted data retrieval method. The field story is not just an incident, an insignificant turn of event, or a mundane conversation. A field story is not just 'background' material in hastily written fieldnotes in computer files or hidden dusty notebooks about trivial specks of social situations. A field story spins experiences about long-term field engagement with peoples and places that lead to feelings of 'being there' and 'being with' those bodies, sites, sounds, tempos, and atmospheres. The editors bring together various anthropologists' elegant voices to showcase the evocative and provocative dimensions of field stories and offer them as pivots for learning moments and vital enlightenments." —Martin F. Manalansan IV, University of Minnesota, Twin Cities

"*Field Stories* brings readers into the hidden corners of intimate experiences that are too often absent from scholarly writings. In a series of deeply personal, often fraught, and always human stories, contributors to this captivating volume revisit old field notes to create original narratives, enriching our understanding of people, places, culture, and history." —Alisse Waterston, John Jay College of Criminal Justice; author of *Light in Dark Times: The Human Search for Meaning*

"*Field Stories* are important stories to tell . . . and for many different reasons. Leggett and Leggett have brought together the kind of rich and compelling tales that rarely find their way into the academic work of ethnographers. Trauma and violence as topics run throughout many of the stories collected in this volume but so, too, does the topic of friendship. The remembrances from the field recounted here demonstrate that ethnographers would do well to find ways to share such stories more often and more broadly." —W. Warner Wood, University of Wisconsin-Milwaukee; author of *Made in Mexico: Zapotec Weavers and the Global Ethnic Art Market*

"The humble act of telling stories is the regenerative seed and solar dynamo that gives energy and substance to anthropology. The essays here offer rich stories and pay careful attention to the places where we share our stories—in the classroom, in the field, and alongside other ethnographers as we learn and practice our craft. This book re-centers storytelling as a crucial resource for anthropological endeavors and should be useful for teaching and for thinking about how we tell our tales from the field." —David Syring, University of Minnesota Duluth

"Anthropologists tell stories. Often, the best are those we tell our students in our classes. The authors, here, bring their emotionally charged stories out of the classroom and into this accessible, readable, and impactful collection. All seasoned ethnographers, they tell of vivid and poignant experience, experimenting with writing while reflecting on the meanings of their tales from the field." —Walter E. Little, University at Albany, SUNY

Field Stories

Field Stories

Experiences, Affect, and the Lessons of Anthropology in the Twenty-First Century

William H. Leggett and Ida Fadzillah Leggett

LEXINGTON BOOKS

Lanham • Boulder • New York • London

Published by Lexington Books
An imprint of The Rowman & Littlefield Publishing Group, Inc.
4501 Forbes Boulevard, Suite 200, Lanham, Maryland 20706
www.rowman.com

6 Tinworth Street, London SE11 5AL, United Kingdom

British Library Cataloguing in Publication Information Available

Library of Congress Cataloging-in-Publication Data

ISBN 9781793643964 (cloth)
ISBN 9781793643988 (pbk)
Library of Congress Control Number: 2020950482

Contents

Introduction

William H. Leggett

One day after class a student approached to apologize for coming in late. "I'm sorry I missed your story," she said. "I heard it was a good one." This encounter left me thinking about the power of a classroom story to engage an audience, while also mulling over questions asked in slight frustration about our anthropological "voice" in the public sphere (or lack thereof). We anthropologists all have personal anecdotes we use in class to explain or elaborate on key ethnographic concepts. We turn to these stories when we want to make a point and make it stick, when we need the tangible to illustrate the abstract. Often these stories are intensely personal. But we use them because we recognize that personal narratives give life to a concept or category or model we want to teach our students. If they work, we keep telling them. They become part of our repertoire. If they don't, we remember them hauntingly. Both sets of stories stay with us.

These field stories are the stuff of anthropology. They explain the work of our lives and why that work is compelling. And yet in the classroom they do much more: they invite an audience in. They create a bond, a connection through which to effectively share information. They are performative experiments designed to entice an ambivalent crowd into hearing and learning something we think is important about the human condition, and an amalgamation of possible ways to view the world. These stories we tell are, in short, an untapped body of knowledge that deserve a wider audience. Of course, they are not our stories alone for they are built on engagement with others. Sometimes these encounters result in a bond in which the "nerve relaxes" and we shed some social armor (Stewart 2007). Other times, these encounters brush up against our own lived realities in ways that make empathy difficult if not impossible (Bourgois 1995). We anthropologists have long reflected on the potentials and problems of our unique kind of social engagement. Yet we too often come to focus on the troubling and self-perpetuating "otherness" of these encounters (Blasco and Hernandez 2012).

An argument could be made that in our attempts to speak to *each other* as anthropologists, we have often edited out our interlocuters from the process. It is as much a problem of writing and publication as it is a problem with our theoretical tool kit. Yet we also recognize another disconnect that is less academically discussed (though certainly emergent in our less-formal get-togethers): in speaking to each other, we often fail to communicate to a larger audience, both outside of anthropology and outside of academia in general. How do we get our body of knowledge, as self-reflexive as it is, as inner-focused as it can sometimes be, as contingent and rabbit-hole-like in our search for solutions, as reliant as it is on "local knowledge" (Geertz 1983), out into the public in a way that might reach an audience and inform that public about what we have collectively accumulated as a discipline concerning social encounter? Do you think Political Scientists suffer this insecurity? Geneticists? Economists? We are a shy discipline.

This book is our attempt to break out of that timidity by promoting the qualitative, the storytelling, and the ethnographic as viable and essential bodies of knowledge to put to use in our ever more connected world. We have all been collecting stories that expose and expand the anthropological canon to reach a popular audience, that illustrate how the things we remember, refer to, rely on in everyday social engagement emerge anew within the moment and reflect beyond; that highlight theoretical insights as a tool kit to be brought to bear in our lives not as an umbrella of overarching explanations, but as an insightful grab-bag to use during contingent encounters; that make explicit the various ways history is present and also contorted in the retelling of current experience; that reveal how ideas and identities ricochet off one another or hit like Western-Apache storytelling-arrows as we navigate the everyday (Basso 1996). As ethnographers, we have learned there are moments of interaction we use to highlight the experience over the model, the forum, the category, the concept, or the frame of reference; that make true that which is emotional and then retold while also challenging the veracity of claims global-to-local observed in the context of conversation, popular discourse, revisionism, or propaganda. We recognize (usually in hindsight) the moments of everyday life that demonstrate the strengths of qualitative analysis as insightful and potentially succinct in ways on par with the quantitative forms of statistics and polls and census data we know too well; that make the case for anthropology's return to the table as an essential voice within the popular discourse. This book focuses on authors/ethnographers/teachers retelling their stories of social encounter both from the field and/or "real life" that provoke enough reflection and insight to become narratives used for successful classroom learning and understanding.

As academics and intellectuals—words we need to respect rather than disparage while moving through the troubling times of the early twenty-first century—we applaud the question-asking introspective aspect of our field, but we also see that there is a potentially positive momentum in inviting a new audience into the anthropological worldview. The authors in this book reclaim the realm of intimate human encounter as a field of study that emphasizes the personal and the experiential as a nexus of real human reaction and emotion from which any number of analyses can emerge (Hoffman 2016; Seremetakis 1994). In short, we propose a more publicly accessible anthropology that plays a more significant part in the public discourse by claiming the ground of personal, face-to-face interaction as a legitimate space of social science analysis too often ignored. My father, a retired professor of literary criticism and newly prolific novelist, once said to me, "There are too many songs about writing songs. And there are too many novels about writing novels." And there may very well be too many ethnographies about writing ethnographies. I cannot argue the opposite. I will posit, however, that the persistence of problems across race, class, gender, sexuality, religious lines (among others) supports a continued perseverance when it comes to understanding essential issues of humans trying to get along with other humans.

As Ruth Behar mused in *The Vulnerable Observer: Anthropology that Breaks Your Heart*, "We are often the witnesses to the worst of humanity but also the thoughtful and empathetic . . . In the retelling of our stories how do we bring the audience along? How do we engage people in the turmoil of our own experiences and those we are engaging with? And how do we share the knowledge we accumulate through these experiences that too often die in the paradoxically parochial world of anthropology" (1996:2)? Anthropology has struggled and at times excelled through periods of colonial, postcolonial, modern, postmodern, feminist, postfeminist, racial, global, and hybrid reflections. Due to these self-evaluations, I believe a more honest discipline has emerged. We are, perhaps more than ever before, better prepared to demonstrate how our popular assumptions should be questioned and evaluated within a social paradigm that emphasizes the qualitative and the narrative, without abandoning the conceptual or theoretical. And, perhaps, we are better equipped to reach out to the world in a way that makes sense not only in relation to our own complicated academic and colonial history but also to a world of non-anthropologists searching for understanding in the world.

Like many in our field we believe it is time to take a more relevant stance in the social sciences and, more importantly, in popular culture, and assert our right to occupy several seats at the table. To accomplish these goals, this book presents a set of narratives that are compelling and revealing, enticing and enlightening. Our approaches to field stories seek to spark excitement for a project of entertaining and informative anthropology that engages the popular imagination while also opening windows into new (and older) ways to view the human condition and the possible answers that lie just beyond our present worldview (Beatty 2019). We bring anthropological analysis to the happenstance of the everyday through anecdotes and thus build on the field of research and writing that examines the role of narrative in the exploration of human understanding (Clifford 1986; Starn 2015). The contributors pay particular attention to the humanistic, personal, ethical, and emergent aspects of human encounters that, due to the mundane familiarity of the story, reach a broader audience. The stories in this book are narrative reproductions of events experienced, considered, publicly presented, and reflected upon before they became the constructions written about here. We, of course, must take hold of the transitions from experiencing to telling to writing as spaces of interrogation worthy of promotion, yet requiring edits, as we move forward with our engagement with the world. But we strive to engage with the story . . . through real stories.

Our reflective impulses are essential to our discipline's development and often lead us down the most insightful rabbit holes. What I argue is that as anthropologists we climb back out of our insulated dens of debate (again), find our public voice, and take advantage of the fact that it is first and foremost in the classroom. The scholastic aspect of anthropological knowledge—the classroom part of the job—is up there with the ethnographic of fieldwork, the historic of primary source searches, the building of citations, and the mining, mincing and overturning of our theoretical deposits. I propose adding to our repertoire a serious examination and promotion of that informal style of narrative construction that takes place most in the classroom, but also around the dinner table and the cocktail party and, now and again, in the conference circuits (Ingold 2018; Rautman 2008; Starn 2015; Stoller 2018; Turner 2007).

Promoting the classroom anecdote as a critical component of our ethnographic work, worthy of building on in order to become better integrated into public discourse, perhaps not surprisingly, requires some defense (Beatty 2019): first, the working out of a narrative so that it reaches ears and draws a response is best done live. Much like a stand-up comedian tests and refines material to small audiences before filming their one-hour specials, the anthropologist tests ideas in conversations with classrooms of students, sometimes even intentionally, before committing our thoughts to paper. The working through of a narrative, the making sense of our own experiences of shared events, and our struggles to see multiple perspectives and contexts are as much classroom performative processes as they are intellectual exercises, prior to becoming textual products.

Second, as we are painfully aware, the anthropologist is often not a gifted writer (Stoller 2018). We fret about writing. We write about writing. We have, at times, become paralyzed by the colonial, racial, gendered, sexualized, economic, religious, and political dynamics of re-presenting "others" as well as ourselves. We express our guilt in texts that simultaneously "give voice to the voiceless" while propelling our own careers upward. We wrestle, more than most, with the fundamental ethics of our chosen careers, studying *ourselves* in our habitats and how to put that work into words. But instead of developing our storytelling bona fides, we have become skilled practitioners in the arts of deflection: hyphenation, strategic "quotation," and the coinage (or disparagement) of "jargon." We continue to swim in the wake of our own outboard engines to the detriment of further outreach and the fulfillment of our promise of informing the public through the eyes of Boas (honestly, not the best writer). In attempts to not get in front of our skis we have without doubt improved our analytical and methodological skill sets while simultaneously losing our audience. Our progress—the living breathing emergent aspects of human engagement that are our discipline's bread and butter—is repeatedly churned beneath the waves of institutional reticence. But one place where the connections continue to get made, where the stories we tell spontaneously become tales with purpose, is the classroom.

It is in the class with students that we tap into the rhythm of a storied emergent. We lecture, converse, debate, and workshop with individuals unschooled in the history of a discipline to which we are tethered but to which they, the students, have no previous connection. Who among us had an anthropology class in high school? We learn to connect our ethnographic experiences to lessons worth sharing because they begin to connect our students to others' lives. Speaking an honest tale that finds shape during semi-Socratic revisions of elaboration and debate, of contextual connection and required concepts, helps us translate these moments of experience into texts that push our anthropological endeavor out into the public realm.

This is not to say we do not already contribute to the scholarly literature and greater understanding of world events and the dynamics of the human condition in ways both large (demographically, historically, and theoretically) and small (intimate, qualitative, narrative-based telling). Where we have been less successful and prolific is in engaging the public in such a way that an anthropological understanding of the world is second nature. As truth is under fire, anthropology provides a long series of tracks toward a better understanding of what goes into "truth," of what we label as real and felt, as propaganda or discourse, of what we feel in our bones and what we file away into the corners of our minds that hold all the academic (and is easily ignored outside the tower). We have become more adept at discovering the multiple realities being lived in our shared geographies —side by side, time by time—sometimes synchronized, sometimes colliding, often in fear of the "other," sometimes in disbelief of ourselves.

The question is, Where is anthropology? To the best of my thinking I believe we strive to tell the truth as we see it while also recognizing the fact that stories can be just that, stories, told and retold, erupting in the moment, lost in the ether or redressed again and again in the vibrations of human encounter. We believe that stories fit narratives in our lives, short term and long term, for better and/or worse, and that verisimilitude matters. There is an authentic to anthropology. We recognize the ways that stories work. The ones we experience and the ones we choose to tell. We are trained in teasing out how stories react to and portray the individual the relational, the local and the global, the past informing the present. It's time to put these skills out into the public.

It is, I would argue, an Us-Them problem at the most base-of-the-spine level. Us and Them is a synapse blockage. In the moment "self" and "other" are quick and easy "file folder" choices we all make, dropping our experiences into prescribed categories. Our job, as anthropologists, is in part to stretch the time, or multiply the synaptic options, in order to help facilitate the potential for connection and empathy. And we do that by sharing stories and deploying our tool kit. Anecdotes—fleshed out in connection to key themes—is the best connective tissue we have come up with so far. The rub is, we are continually asking students to put themselves in another's shoes and work through the ethnocentric struggles that interfere with that process. Yet, in this set of stories we ourselves are gazing inward, saying, "this is what happened to me." So this is an idea still trying to realize itself. But what we are doing is not navel-gazing, with its emphasis on stagnant reflection. Rather, what our perspective provides is a Point Zero at which the reader can come to see the perspectives, emotions, and thoughts of the fieldworker (as well as the anthropologically-trained living their everyday life), and from these points we encourage movement and outward momentum, drawing the field site, or any moment of encounter, as a series of fluid connections and interconnections, and the fieldworkers as ones who draw the field and are also drawn into the field. This approach emphasizes culture as kinetic not static. And engagement as social, not singular.

In this book, we have assembled a set of accessible, engaging, enlightening essays that take face-to-face human engagement as a place to begin. There is a frame that holds these together. What came out of these articles, maybe not surprisingly, was a sort of antipathy/empathy dichotomy. Are we friends? Are we divided by purpose? Is my job as an anthropologist interfering with my ability to connect? Is your concern about how you will be represented making you reticent to share? These are timeless debates in anthropology. But they might be timely in our currently "Balkanized" circumstances.

While what unites the chapters in this book is the storied classroom aspect of their origins, there are also conceptual strands tying the pieces to one another. One such strand running through several chapters is the importance of affect on our individual educations. There are different synonyms used to touch on a concept many of us probably first became aware of through the work of Kathleen Stewart (1996, 2017) or perhaps started to percolate with the Rosaldos (Rosaldo 1980, 1989): emotion and heart, resonance, emotional states, spectacles, pleasures, sense(s), anxiety, panic, wonder, and ease (for more recent examples see Rautman 2008; Stainova 2019). These words take us into a world of emotional engagement or disconnect and the discomfort of working through these emotions while relying on an ethnographic toolbox of social encounter originally developed and put to use in the most dispassionate of ways in an attempt to speak to the scientific objectivity of the time. Bridging this emotional gap so lacking in the social sciences appears an implicit agenda in a number of our chapters.

Another strand focused on by the authors is friendship. Several chapters in this book explore the intimacy and antipathy of fieldwork: of living life with and through others while also conducting research that speaks of and for these others without them present in the writing; of participating while observing; of befriending and then departing; of leaving people behind after perhaps the most intense interactions of our lives. Mains, for example, in his recollections from fieldwork in Ethiopia, brings to life the wealth disparities inherent in our ethnographic projects and how over time and distance, class differences are exacerbated instead of dissipated through participant observation. Pardue sheds light on the ways our imagined selves and others, full as they are of pop-culture and history references, can serve as obstacles to understanding and intimacy in a piece that travels with him from Alabama to Brazil. Glaros examines ways that friendships and secrets intertwine in her Greek fieldsite. And Elliot describes a violent and traumatic event in Kenya that happened with the blurring of lines between acquaintances, friends, locals, and neighbors. A final strand is the quest to find the proper tone and language to express often painful and difficult moments. The authors did not merely share their stories; they also experimented with different ways to express difficult things. Some chapters have a more fictionalized and creative voice, while others used a more intimate academic language. Each writer brought their own voice to the table, finding a tone most appropriate for their own story.

For example, Pintar relies on poetic forms to capture the voices of those newly recovered from the war in Croatia, while Ida Leggett falls back on field notes from fieldwork in Thailand to capture her observations of children's encounters with violence. And in my own chapter I play with a more creative side of language to better capture the effect of space and travel on our identities, using a train ride across the United States as my vehicle.

I wish the chapters to speak for themselves, but I will say a few things by way of introduction. Each author came to the project with varying degrees of comfort toward this intimate reflection. Some of us considered ourselves fairly introspective only to discover we were not. Others, concerned they were not capturing the context of their environment well enough, revealed themselves in ways that surprised both the author and the editors. We all learned from each other in the process, interrogating questions like: How do relationships change over time? How do our proposed research projects become secondary to the everyday encounters of ethnographic fieldwork? How do friendships become altered through the changing circumstances of power, economic, racial dynamics of ethnographic engagement as we are living our lives while also participating in and observing the lives of others? Are we, as cultural anthropologists, exploiting others' often difficult lives for our own benefits? How well do our ethnographic methods work to navigate the everyday? How do we express the painful revelations of the field? Key themes emerge along the way: friendships are contingent but meaningful. Time in a place matters because time plus place plus a steep learning curve makes for sometimes dramatic transitions.

Writing is an experiment in communication. As is music. As is comedy. Trauma comes in all shades, from the mundane to the explosive. All of these emotional and intellectual insights are often left on the table as we construct our academic conclusions to our fieldwork experiences. Here we try to capture some of the beauty and despair in the uncertainty of the moment; the moments that stayed with us long after the research was done and the articles were published. These are the stories we hold onto and that we decide at some point to share with our students.

The women and men of this book are all experienced qualitative field researchers, and have been teaching students for many years. Each author focused on topics that a typical audience would not even think of as "anthropological," since they do not fit nicely into our traditional categories, while demonstrating just how anthropological these experiences truly are. Further, the divisions between "us" and "them" are a constant point for reflective analysis throughout the chapters. In the end, we hope readers get a sense that these stories, while highly readable, were not easily told. The writing process is a difficult one. We, the editors, thank our contributors for making it look easy.

So, to end where I began, after class one day a student approached to apologize for coming in late. "I'm sorry I missed your story," she said. "I heard it was a good one." While I do not know whether the story was good, she did hear about it. And it just might have left a feeling of wanting to know more. Her comment left me thinking about the power of a classroom story to engage an audience. And as anthropologists, I believe we need to think more about that aspect of our discipline.

REFERENCES

Basso, Keith. 1996. *Wisdom Sits in Places: Landscape and Language among the Western Apache*. Albuquerque: University of New Mexico Press.

Beatty, Andrew. 2019. *Emotional Worlds: Beyond an Anthropology of Emotion*. Cambridge: Cambridge University Press.

Behar, Ruth. 1996. *The Vulnerable Observer: Anthropology That Breaks Your Heart*. Boston, MA: Beacon Press.

Gay y Blasco, Paloma and Liria de la Cruz Hernández. 2012. "Friendship, Anthropology." *Anthropology and Humanism*, 37(1): 1–14.

Bourgois, Phillippe. 1995. *In Search of Respect: Selling Crack in El Barrio* (Structural Analysis in the Social Sciences), 2nd Edition. New York, NY: Cambridge University Press.

Clifford, James and George Marcus. 1986. *Writing Culture: The Poetics and Politics of Ethnography*. Berkley, CA: University of California Press.

Hoffman, Diane M. 2016. "Learning to See: Intuition and Perception in Fieldwork in Haiti." *Anthropology and Humanism*, 41(1): 28–38.

Ingold, Timothy. 2018. *Anthropology: Why It Matters*. Cambridge, UK: Polity Press.

Geertz, Clifford. 1983. *Local Knowledge*. New York, NY: Basic Books.

Rosaldo, Michelle Zimbalist. 1980. *Knowledge and Passion: Illongot Notions of Self and Social Life*. Cambridge, MA: Cambridge University Press.

Rosaldo, Renato. 1989. *Culture and Truth: The Remaking of Social Analysis*. Boston, MA: Beacon Press.

Rautman, Alison. 2008. "Thick Description of a Visit Home: In Tribute to Clifford Geertz." *Anthropology and Humanism*, 33(1/2): 85–94.

Seremetakis, C. Nadia. 1994. *The Senses Still: Perception and Memory as Material Culture in Modernity*. Chicago, IL: University of Chicago Press.

Stainova, Yana. 2019. "Enchantment as Method." *Anthropology and Humanism*, 44(2): 214–230.

Starn, Orin. 2015. "Introduction." In *Writing Culture and the Life of Anthropology*, edited by Orin Starn, 1–24. Durham, NC: Duke University Press.

Stewart, Kathleen. 1996. *A Space on the Side of the Road: Cultural Poetics in an "Other" America*. Princeton, NJ: Princeton University Press.

_____. 2017. "In the World that Affect Proposed." *Cultural Anthropology*, 32(2): 192–198.

Stoller, Paul. 2018. *Adventures in Blogging: Public Anthropology and Popular Media*. Ontario: University of Toronto Press.

Turner, Edith. 2007. "Introduction to the Art of Ethnography." *Anthropology and Humanis*, 32(2): 108–116.

Chapter 1

Children and the Experience of Mundane Violence

Unexpected Stories from the Field

Ida Fadzillah Leggett

INTRODUCTION

Sometimes we are fortunate to experience moments that turn our worldview upside down and change us forever. These moments can be big—the birth of a child, for example—but more often they are small and unexpected, and they transform us into "before" and "after" versions of ourselves.

As an anthropologist who has ventured into fieldwork and back again, I now try to magically transport my own students to the wonder of the field-site with vivid stories of the unexpected. And I find myself returning to the same tales that are guaranteed to hook my audience: I notice that the students sit up straighter and lean in while their eyes grow big. Once the story—always short and often colorful, matching the characteristics of the Western Apache tales recounted by Basso (1996)—is over, there is often a silence followed by an ever-louder buzz of excited conversation as students talk with and over each other. Once calmed, they then ask questions they sincerely want answered: "What did you do?" "Why did they do that?" "How did you know how to respond?" After my own answers, I would often throw the question back: "What would YOU do in that situation? Why? What would you have done differently? How do you know what to do? What would have stopped you from doing that?" And after a pause, even the quiet ones would engage with this remembered world with thoughtfulness and sincerity, and the students would leave the classroom that day transformed at least a little, as if they had walked through a door into another world.

Behind the podium I find myself transported back to these field moments, and realize all over again why the anthropological endeavor is so difficult to adequately describe and yet so important to our understanding of the lived experience. "Culture," our theoretical bread and butter, is firmly ensconced not simply in behaviors, beliefs, objects, ideas, or traditions; it is also found in the mundane and everyday, as well as in aspirations and feelings. Additionally, culture is very much a subject of movement and flux: of the flow of days and nights, of trial and error and frustrations and revelations, and of hopes and desires that often strike us as unremarkable. These persistent fieldwork stories, these oral presentations of vivid images that engage with some of the movement and flux, demonstrate that we don't really capture these field moments: rather, they capture us.

As teachers of anthropology, we often try to share these unexpected and vexing moments with our students because we see the value of such affect-laden experiences, and we also see the value of a good fieldwork story that captures the brightness of the field. We use simple, clear language—unlike the language of our regular lectures that tend to be more verbose and jargon-laden—to draw listeners into a different space and a different time, and with it into a different mindset or "alternative stance" (Hoffman 2016, 280) toward the new and the different. And as we teach our students the tenets of anthropology, we also instill in them the importance of the nuts and bolts of the anthropological perspective, for "classroom spaces should not be underes-timated—it is here in the trenches where the local phenomenon is reproduced and reinforced" (Falcone 2013, 126).

We recognize that we are strengthened by the unexpected and the emo-tional, for they always teach us something valuable. As Starn notes, "Our fieldwork is always caught somewhere in between all too predictable dis-coveries and moments of something like genuine learning and sometimes even revelation. The trouble is that we're not always able to tell just which is which" (2015, 6). Beatty (2019) suggests that what is needed to explore these moments "is a form of writing that captures dimensions of life too often left to fiction, parceled out among experts in other fields, or left out of the account altogether; something like that narrative and imaginative engagement that enables the historical to make the past present. Our challenge, as anthropolo-gists, is to make the *present* present" (12). I would hazard that these moments of revelation, our efforts to "make the *present* present" for our students, are often the impetus behind much of our most popular classroom story-tellings.

To interrogate our own frame of interpretation of the world is to acknowl-edge that various factors come into play that influence and craft one's perspective, questions, and conclusions. This is an anthropological skill: developing the ethnographic perspective allows the researcher to understand a culture beyond its postcard symbolism. While difficult, the fieldworker learns to adjust her frame and focus outward and upward and move with the society's flows of time. She then refocuses her Western-trained eyes on the areas of significance the people themselves know to be important, and dives into those areas and unpacks even more detail, in order to frame the moment in a way that can be publicly shared and understood. This chapter examines examples from my own dissertation fieldwork conducted a lifetime ago, focusing on two moments that haunt me to this day and that have morphed into retellings that generations of students have heard and (hopefully) taken to heart. As an anthropologist of childhood and youth, I learned more about children's lives from these two incidences than I did from all the library research or interviews gleaned in the field. And in sharing them with students in the classroom, I have learned even more.

FIELD STORIES

I engaged in my first fieldwork experience while working on my dissertation project in Northern Thailand from 1996–1998. I was twenty-seven years old, newly married, and childless. My research centered on rural teenage girls. I wanted to better understand how these girls thought about their "life strategy narratives": namely, how they perceived their possible future lives. With the help of local admininstrators and a senior monk in the nearby Buddhist temple, I found myself in a medium-sized village renting space in the home of a local family who gave me their main bedroom (while they all moved into their seven-year-old son's room), and provided me three delicious meals a day. The village was relatively prosperous, with a hospital, dentist, and district administrative headquarters. But this place also hid a dark reality: not only was this geographic area—known euphemistically as the Golden Triangle—on the route of illicit drugs like heroin and amphetamines out of Myanmar, but, also, I soon discovered, never before had these drugs been so potent, cheap, or readily available.

To capture complex village life as lived by the children I came to know, it was necessary to lift the veil of "official" Northern Thai rural life and dis-cover the "backstage" reality different from the touristic, static, and pastoral images (and the corresponding image of Thai villagers as individuals within a homogenized "ethnographic present") perpetuated in colorful brochures as well as in older ethnographies of the region (e.g, see Embree 1950; Hanks 1962; Kingshill 1965). These moments when the pretty veil was lifted were often unsettling, but did much to explain how children experienced and understood their own lives. The most memorable aspects of my fieldwork experience were those moments that were the most jarring, and I find myself sharing these vignettes frequently with my students to drive home the "truths" that are revealed in the field. My first story comes from a moment that occurred about six months into my research, at the village elementary school.

Vignette One

The elementary school, which also housed a preschool, was a series of well-maintained single-story wooden buildings with only one small building—the headmaster's office attached to the school's one-room library—air-conditioned. The grounds were well swept and cared for by the students themselves, and the elementary school had a total of 477 students, with 23 students in each of the 2 grade six classes I observed. They wore starched white button-down short-sleeved shirts, and either pleated skirts or long shorts in navy blue with white sneakers. When they took their shoes off before entering the classroom, I noticed that several had holes in their socks.

Among the twelve-year-olds, I divided my time between the two sixth-grade classes. In the first classroom I observed, there was a beautiful view of the rice fields and the mountains. There was a cooler full of water and the students would get up and help themselves whenever they were thirsty. I wrote in my field notes from Monday, May 19, "The classroom smells vaguely of dead rat. There is a nice breeze blowing through the big windows, but it is noisy because of the loud talking coming from the adjoining class. The students don't seem to mind." At lunch I would follow the girls who had taken me under their wing, and sit with them in a *sala*—outdoor covered patios—while they shared their lunches of sticky rice and grilled meats with each other, playing with the preschool children, dressing each others' hair with flowers, or pressing flame of the forest petals onto their nails like scarlet claws. We would often go *"pay thiaw"* or "travel" around the school, buy a cheap dessert of ice-cream and then get our toothbrushes to brush our teeth at the faucet in the yard behind the classroom before class resumed.

During one lunch period, when I was tired of the interactions and excited conversations and tugging on my hands to follow the girls here and there and woefully behind on my field-note transcriptions, I decided to remain in the classroom to write up my thoughts of the day. I sat in the back of the room with its wooden walls and dirt floor, its posters of Thai kings, its chalkboard, and reveled in the silence of a few quiet minutes to myself. However, I was not alone in the classroom: about five boys had remained in the room to eat their lunch and then to goof around, and they completely ignored me like I was part of the furniture. These twelve-year-olds ate their boxed lunches quickly, cleaned up, and began to play. They were noisy and happy, and then the energy level became concentrated as they pushed back some chairs and tables from the front of the room. I was confused by what they were doing, never having focused my observations on boys behavior before, and began to pay attention. One boy took a piece of white chalk from the blackboard, picking a sizeable specimen not yet reduced by constant use. He pulled out a penknife and sliced up the chalk producing a series of flat little circular pieces. He then carved a straight line down the middle of each slice, revealing an end-result that looked remarkably like pills. Then all the boys pretended they were ingesting the tablets, yelling *"Yaa baa! Yaa baa!"* ("crazy pills" in Thai, the colloquial name for a common type of amphetamine). They then began acting as if high on speed, laughing and attacking each other, falling down, and weaving unsteadily around the room. All in all the boys had great fun, but I was shocked and speechless.

There had been a large and constant supply of amphetamines—and amphetamine users—in the village for years. It has become enculturated into the village culture, and now children were growing up playing "addict." I use this story in my classroom to explore more closely how everyday acts of mundane violence become normalized in a community and to push my students to understand how changes become routine in the time-span of one generation.

This is a solid example of how field truths can appear during the most unexpected times, and we are surprised, appalled, and delighted at being able to observe human truths reveal themselves. But there are other moments harder to reconcile, which are unexpected in stressful and painful ways and that I would argue are also part and parcel of the fieldwork experience.

The following vignette is not a story I have shared in writing or formal academic presentations, because its intimate experience lends itself best to more personal spaces of discussion and verbal connection. But I reach for it again and again every semester, and I find that it works every time to draw students into the frame of the ethnographic endeavor, and causes students to sincerely ponder concepts of violence and of ethics in the field better than any reading assignment. There was an incident, a moment actually, that has stayed with me over twenty years later. It was a short moment, no longer than four minutes, but it has made an impact on me personally, on my studies of childhood, and on my teachings for my own students.

Vignette Two

It was May 5, 1997, and a national holiday. There was thus no school, which freed me of classroom observations. I decided to walk to my friend Mei's video store to interview her. She was a woman in her late 20s like me, and she lived with her boyfriend in a long, low building that had been converted into multiple apartments. The units enjoined in a line of single-story apartments, and each were characterized by a large garage door at the front that rolled up into the ceiling and opened into the main living area. It looked like a long row of garages, with large wide driveways leading to the door. People used these doors as entranceways to their apartments, or to their shops. Beyond the main room was a bathroom, a bedroom, and a space that could be used for cooking.

And then there was a door leading out to a small back yard. You could always tell when someone was home because the garage door would be wide open.

When I arrived I was disappointed to find that Mei had gone to the nearby village of Wiang Chai with a friend. Her boyfriend was there; he was not sure when she would be back, but he told me to stay and wait for her. He raided their video shelves and started "Escape from LA" with Kurt Russell on the television to entertain me; when that ended and Mei had still not returned, he offered to put "The Sacketts" on. I said, no, I would just sit outside and catch up on my writing.

On this early afternoon, it was bright and sunny and hot, and I settled down to wait for Mei in one of two white plastic chairs ubiquitous to Thai open-air restaurants that were perched along the side of her driveway. The chairs were backed up against a concrete wall about six feet tall that extended along each property line from the house down to the street. The wall was not thick, but at least afforded each household the feeling of privacy. As I sat and waited, I wrote in my notebook some thoughts about the previous week and waited some more. Then I heard the stirring of the neighbors whose apartment was on the other side of the wall behind me. They were a hill tribe—Akha—couple (one of several in the village) with a young son who was about seven years old. At night they sold "hill tribe" carvings to the tourists at the Night Bazaar, though they had told me previously that the carvings were actually mass-produced, and then aged by them in their backyard. During the day the husband worked another job while the wife took care of the needs of their son. I loved the wife (I had never met the husband) because she was kind and happy to talk to me, and her smile was always wide and genuine.

This is what I wrote in my field notes later that day after I returned to my own house: "I was sitting with my back to the wall, and all the noises were happening behind me. I heard everything like it was happening right in front of me. This was the first time I was so physically affected by something that was not actually happening to me; the kid was screaming, and I could hear each whack, and they all sounded like hard slaps. I thought I was going to throw up, but they would not stop. The woman just kept yelling at the kid who just kept screaming 'It's enough!' It was over in a couple of minutes but felt like an eternity, and I had to go home after that."

When I think back, the details are more vivid than the notes reveal, because I couldn't bring myself to fully express everything that happened. The events felt magnified too because I could not see any of it, and the sounds I heard from the other side of the wall left a lot to the imagination. I could not bring myself to name the child, but in my notes simply called him "kid."

These are the details I replay over and over in my mind: the mother was yelling at her son, screaming at the top of her lungs. She sounded unhinged, as uncontrolled as a person could sound, and he was crying and screaming

"I'm sorry! I'm sorry!" I was frozen in place, I didn't know what was going on, because I was not yet fluent in the Akha dialect, I could not understand what she was saying to him. My heart started pounding, and I started sweating, and still I remained frozen. There was a chase, and I heard the mother hit the boy with a belt—*thwap!*—and he screamed, "I'm sorry, I'm sorry!" And still I heard the belt come down again, and again, and again. And still I sat and did nothing, like my limbs did not work, or my brain could not function. And perhaps that was what was happening: we all need our cultural "code" to set our functions—even physical movements, apparently—and without that guidance we don't know what to do. I knew that in this village this type of discipline was common and accepted, but I had never seen it happen before. And even growing up, I had never in my own life ever been witness to such a beating, or such anger, or such terror. So was it ok here? Should I do something? What? Should I say something? What? Never had I felt so immobile, rooted in place because I did not know what to do next.

The action moved back into the house, which of course I did not see. Rather I heard the sounds get softer and the door close. And yet I still did not move. Do I call the police, who were some of the most corrupt individuals in the village? Do I find the father? What do I do? In this moment of short-circuit, I did the only thing my body understood to do—I went home and locked myself in my bedroom for the afternoon.

I went back to the apartments later, and found my friend Mei and apologized for not being there when she returned. And then I went to her neighbor's house to check on the boy. He was there, running around chasing after another little boy and laughing and playing like today was any other day. And his mother was as smiling and welcoming as she had always been. And I smiled, and made small talk, and was relieved. But I was also angry at myself for not doing something, and perhaps even more angry at my anthropologist self for understanding at the level of my very body that actions and reactions are culturally driven, and need to be considered carefully.

I am sure there are a lot of people out there who will read this account and say they would definitely have stepped in, they would have definitely confronted the mother, they would definitely have taken the belt away from her, or they would definitely have called the police. My response to that is "you were not there." Righteous anger is easy in hypothetical situations. But confronting it when it is right in front of you (or in my case, behind me) is more difficult, more complicated situation. I was young, alone, and living in a foreign country. I had no family or social connections or safe space in the village, my language skills were only "good enough," and my social skills were, at best, awkward.

But I knew at that moment that a child was involved and that he was being hurt, even if it was just for a short while. I do not know if my inaction was the right move and I still do not know. But what I do know is that to this day, my embodied experience that day of fear, panic, and confusion taught me more about the power of culture than anything I have experienced since. Four minutes. That was how long the entire incident probably took. Four minutes that taught me an important lesson about what it means to be human, and has stayed with me far longer than most other parts of my fieldwork. Why was it so visceral, a moment that carved itself into my sense of myself not only as an anthropologist, but as a human being? And I still feel haunted by the guilt of not doing something, anything, and vow that if I am ever confronted with a similar situation I would finally act.

The most problematic aspect of this moment was that it shook my sense of self as a good human being. As the sounds began, I froze. And I realize I would have frozen if I had heard these sounds anywhere in the world, whether in the context of my work or in my own apartment building back home. Sounds of strikes, of screams, of cries, of silence, would have caused me to freeze. To know that I am not a hero but a deer in the headlights is not something I can gracefully accept. I have also come to understand that a moment does not define a person, though perhaps the actions that come after most certainly do. I checked in on the poor boy later, checked in on his mother, and made sure they were both of sound mind and body. I assuaged my guilt as best I could, realized that sounds without images amplify the imagination, and that if I had gotten up—shaky legs and all—and had confronted the situation, I might have made the situation worse for everyone involved.

Four minutes and the power and experience of mundane violence were revealed to me in slow motion. Mundane violence shades the everyday experiences of everyone in a society in ways that leave scars that remind but are perhaps too ugly to be acknowledged. It is also something that crosses international borders and doesn't remain within linguistically distinct societies. A child is being hurt by his own parents—punished or spanked. That happens everywhere and cannot be escaped. How do I make sense of it? I try to understand it, and I try to understand myself by sharing the story.

I think retelling this memory teaches my students that emotions (my own and that of my Thai community) reveal truths rather than cloud facts about the society. Concepts and experiences such as love and fear tell us much about cultures, about how the people within these places see themselves and make their decisions. And while these affective aspects of society do not fit into a neat category like "religion" or "social organization," they are significant aspects of the culture as well as our fieldwork experiences. As a field story I tell in my classroom, this narrative is part confessional, part life lesson: reality is so much harder to categorize than the books make it seem. First, fieldwork is not always, if ever, clear-cut, and the ethics surrounding any one moment can be blurry. When I ask my students to think about how they would have responded in this situation, their responses are generally thoughtful and honest as they break out of textbook mode and actually place themselves in another cultural and social situation. And while they never agree with the "right" course of action, they clearly realize that the different reactions are all ways of trying to deal with life lived in incremental moments in the "best" way given the circumstances.

Second, my students learn that faraway village life is not always peaceful, and families are not always sheltering. Dangers can come from the inside and can be perceived as more threatening than the dangers of an unknown life far away. The children in this village, both boys and girls, were leaving as soon as they finished secondary school and going to the big cities of Bangkok and beyond to work in factories and orchards and brothels in Taiwan, Israel, and Germany. It would be incomplete to frame this exodus—especially into the particularly dangerous work of prostitution that the girls in this region are funneled into—as solely one of economic desperation or ignorance or forced labor. A more complete picture demonstrates that life in a peaceful village can be anything but, and youth leaving for urban unknowns could also be an insight into the power of emotion and desire pushing youth to leave an area of mundane violence to try their luck elsewhere.

ANALYSIS: THE POWER OF THE STORY

The ethnographic field, along with our own everyday lives, is simply—and complexly—life as lived. There is no impenetrable border there between public and private life, between working and playing (Gmelch and Gmelch 2018, 2), or even between structure and perceived chaos. And for me, I am working to better understand how this field knowledge is sometimes best transmitted to the layman—be they students or the general public—through "nonconventional" means like stories, blog posts, podcasts, poetry, art, performances, music, films, or fiction. But at the center of it all, tying it all together, is the significance of a good story. I agree with Paul Stoller (2018) who states, "No matter the format, works that remain open to the world are usually those in which writers use narratives—stories—to connect with their readers. Those are the texts that endure, texts, that people may well be reading 10, 20, or even 50 years after their initial publication" (xvii). He concludes "For me, our capacity to imagine, create, anticipate, and speculate about the social world emerges from a central source: the story" (194).

From these experiences and their subsequent retellings, I have come to understand that the power of the story stems from its ability to transcend the self-other binary by inviting the reader into the everyday world of encounter, enchantment, and wonder, challenging us to see beyond the curtain of predictable patterns and expectations. And I would argue that this affective analysis of culture is as important as any other, for we are largely creatures of affect: our emotions, fears, desires, aspirations, all that is unseen but deeply felt drive many of our most important decisions. I believe that this perspective on affect is an important aspect of understanding culture, or as Berlant and Stewart (2019) put it, the "ordinaries" of life that "stage a high-intensity tableau of the way things are or could become" (5). And the intensity of the vignettes examined here can also be found in their structure as stories about stories actively layered in their presentation: from the actual events, to the vivid memories, through the back-and-forth of classroom discussions, to this recounting to a whole new audience over the pages of text rather than voices. This layering is a way field stories are given heft and imbued with so much significance.

I believe we are interested in telling a good story, because a good story can transmit important truths sometimes faster than dry academic prose. Edith Turner (2007) believed that storytelling was of high importance in anthropology (113), stating that "we have all noted how when a writer starts telling a story that is at the core of her ethnography, her writing becomes delightful, lucid, and flowing" (109). She contrasted this form to theoretical analysis and found the latter to be much less delightful. Dennis Tedlock (2004) called these two kinds of anthropological writing "the human, and the rigid," and preferred the former. For Edith Turner, "Ethnographic stories are like sacred stories in that they are told because they are true and because anthropologists know they will throw light on humanity's knowledge of itself" (114). At the same time, what anthropologists often confront in the field (as well as in everyday life) play out like a good story. For Rautman (2008), "There are events in our lives that can take on the proportions of an epic tale, a saga, existing in mythic time and space. We sort out the jumble of events into a narrative framework, with commentary, highlighting first one aspect, then another. The tale becomes legendary, each version of the telling slightly altered to fit the audience, but like all mythic tales, each version equally valid (85)." Through our own small epic tales we lead our listeners to another space, and we use our stories to open the portal. We invite them to step into another world, and we step through the gateway together.

REFERENCES

Basso, Keith. 1996. *Wisdom Sits in Places: Landscape and Language among the Western Apache*. Albuquerque: University of New Mexico Press.

Beatty, Andrew. 2019. *Emotional Worlds: Beyond an Anthropology of Emotion*. Cambridge: Cambridge University Press.

Berlant, Lauren and Kathleen Stewart. 2019. *The Hundreds*. Durham, NC: Duke University Press.

Embree, John F. 1950. "Thailand—A Loosely Structured System." *American Anthropologist*, 52: 181–193.

Falcone, Jessica Marie. 2013. "The Hau of Theory: The Kept-Gift of Theory Itself in American Anthropology." *Anthropology and Humanism*, 38(2): 122–145.

Gmelch, George and Sharon Bohn Gmelch. 2018. *In the Field: Life and Work in Cultural Anthropology*. Berkeley, CA: University of California Press.

Hanks, Lucien M. 1962. "Merit and Power in the Thai Social Order." *American Anthropologist*, 64: 1247–1259.

Hoffman, Diane M. 2016. "Learning to See: Intuition and Perception in Fieldwork in Haiti." *Anthropology and Humanism*, 41(1): 28–38.

Kingshill, Konrad. 1965. *Ku Daeng: The Red Tomb*. Bangkok: Christian College Publishers.

Rautman, Alison E. 2008. "Thick Description of a Visit Home: In Tribute to Clifford Geertz." *Anthropology and Humanism*, 33(1): 85–94.

Starn, Orin. 2015. "Introduction." In *Writing Culture and the Life of Anthropology*, edited by Orin Start, 1–24. Durham, NC: Duke University Press.

Stoller, Paul. 2018. *Adventures in Blogging: Public Anthropology and Popular Media*. Toronto: University of Toronto Press.

Tedlock, Dennis. 2004. "Voices in Ethnographic Writing." *Statement for the Writing Culture Planning Seminar*, School of American Research, Santa Fe, NM, October 28–29.

Turner, Edith. 2007. "Introduction to the Art of Ethnography." *Anthropology and Humanism*, 32(2): 108–116.

Chapter 2

Stories from the *Other* Notebooks

The Poetics of Encounter in Postwar Croatia

Judith Pintar

Explain to me
  what
  he slaps the table
  is the point of poetry?
She loves this story
  her husband, the ship captain
  slapping the table
  what
  is the use of a poem

When I went to Croatia in the 1990s to study postwar recovery, I kept field notebooks in which I recorded research-related plans, observations, interviews, translations, and analyses, with a specific focus on women's experiences in war. In a different notebook (which over a year and half grew to be several notebooks and journals), it was my habit to set down in ink my personal experiences that seemed, at least initially, to be unrelated to my research. I recorded daily my conversations with friends, acquaintances, family members, and strangers in Zagreb and Dubrovnik where I lived for extended periods between 1997 and 1999, and in my travels to Bosnia, Slovenia, Serbia, and other parts of Croatia where I attended conferences and visited my relatives. Because my research notes were gendered, in the sense that was centered almost completely on the lives of women, my *other* notebooks became an inadvertent repository for the encounters that I had with men. Some of these experiences were positive and enlightening; others were aggressive and unwelcome. I recorded my reflections on them all.

The casual conversations that I had in the field often ranged toward people's memories of the war, though I made it a point not to ask people direct personal questions about its effects on their lives. This was more than politeness. The ethics of researching in war zones is complicated (Boyden 2004). There was a story going around when I was in the field about a journalist who stood on a table in a Bosnian refugee camp and called out, "Anyone here who was raped and speaks English?" This was fully believable, even if the tale originated in a refugee camp in the Congo in 1960 (Abdela 2007; Behr 1985). Many times, I heard people angrily describe western academics and journalists as predatory war tourists, only living in the country to make careers from the suffering of others. Although this charge was never specifically directed at me, I took the criticism in and I wrestled with it, along with other ethical challenges associated with studying war (Clark 2012; Huisman 2008).

In addition to the field study component of my dissertation, it was also a theoretical critique of psychiatric diagnostic instruments—developed to study the effects of trauma of individuals—which were widely and uncritically applied to people traumatized in war. I had written about the secondary trauma associated with ahistorical and decontextualized humanitarian intervention in war zones, so I was well aware that I could through my ignorance cause harm, even if it was my intention to do good (Pintar 2000; Stubbs and Soroya 1996; Cushman 2004). I was particularly concerned with protecting people's privacy, especially important because I was studying trauma. It is nearly impossible to anonymize personal stories in a small town, village, or neighborhood where everyone can guess who was interviewed based on the smallest details. And one cannot really whip out an IRB-approved consent form while sharing a pitcher of beer with friends and acquaintances in the evening when the conversation gets interesting. So, the casual conversations that I recorded in my *other* notebooks I thought of as personal experiences rather than research-related material that I was collecting, with the intent to analyze and publish.

Over time, of course, it became clear to me that I was learning much more about the country and its people and the war from personal encounters than from my formal interviews and focus groups. This is quite a pedestrian observation in an anthropological context, an expectable outcome of participant observation. But long-term qualitative fieldwork was an uneasy method for a sociologist to adopt during the "Quant-Qual" wars of the 1990s. What constituted valid, reliable, accurate, and ethical data were issues of contention from both sides of that methodological divide. Eventually, my project pivoted to include community-based participatory research which allowed me to write about experiences to which I was a direct witness, as well as to give back something to the community I studied (Torbert 2000; Özerdem and Bowd 2016).

My research questions evolved while I was in the field, in part because of what I learned in focus groups and interviews, but also, as a result of casual conversations, recorded in my *other* notebooks. In the end, the boundaries I had established between the two text streams were porous; information, insight, and emotion flowed between them. My non-research encounters had informed my understanding of the region and had become part of me in ways that were impossible to tease apart. Nonetheless, the two-notebook system continued when I returned from the field because it remained true that the notes I had taken in my *other* notebooks were not data in a sociologically acceptable sense. I had no idea what I should do with what I had written there. And I had a bigger problem. In the years following my dissertation defense I struggled with how to turn my research into a published monograph, given the unlikelihood of a resolution of the ethical and privacy issues that inevitably arise when researching war trauma.

The book I eventually wrote was a sociocultural history of hypnosis (Pintar and Lynn 2008). It fell well within the larger circle of my research interest in psychiatric history, but was tangentially, if at all, related to my original fieldwork. Yes, I punted. The choice to write a different book relieved the pressure to publish. It gave me more time to reflect on what I had learned in the field and what I was supposed to do with the truths that people had so generously given to me while I was there. I was truly and deeply stuck, but three small epiphanies gave me a path forward.

THE FIRST EPIPHANY

A call for papers came from the Slavic studies journal *Ulbandus*, which was hosting a special issue entitled "The Wound and the Imagination—Aesthetics of Violence in Slavic Art." I understood they were looking for contributions that analyzed artistic expressions originating in the region that used violent imagery to explore historical and contemporary traumas. I could have sent them something on post-Yugoslav cinema, a topic that interested me; however, my mind also leaped to my *other* notebooks. It occurred to me that the non-scholarly, free-form, and emotionally engaged way in which I had recorded the stories that men had told me made them read like poetry. In fact, I had formatted many of them *as* poetry.

Looking back, I think that I did this because I wanted to capture not just *what* I heard but *how I had heard it*. In many cases, the lines I chose to record in verse were taken from longer conversations. They expressed the heart of what people most wanted me to know. This is not unlike pulling from an interview the single passage needed to support a theoretical point in an academic paper. But there is a key difference. These conversational snippets that I formatted as poetry arose from encounters—not interviews. They were the result of a two-way sharing of ideas and life experiences, mine as well as theirs. I would not have recorded these stories in my academic fieldnotes because of concern over "contamination" of the qualitative data (Kirkevold and Bergland 2007; Moyle 2002). These encounters weren't about me, but they included me; in my poetic expression of them, I was never excised from the frame.

His mother asked him not to be afraid
and so he put his fear away
now he can't remember what the truth is
We sit with the question between us
on the table with the drinks
when it has been your duty to lose yourself
how do you get yourself back?

I decided, on a whim, to submit to *Ulbandus* a collection of poetry gleaned from my *other* notebooks, based on the writing that had captured the voices, stories, and lives of men with whom I had shared conversations. At that time, publishing poetry based on my fieldwork felt like a risky, career-killing professional choice. But I was between full-time academic positions, and I had the freedom to take risks that I couldn't have afforded if I were trying to make a case for my tenure in sociology. The notebook entries were edited and became poetry almost effortlessly. In keeping with their "Aesthetics of Violence" theme, the poems I chose to submit to *Ulbandus* were those that most directly addressed the war. In the brief introduction to the collection, which I had entitled "feminine nouns that end in a consonant: conversations with Croatian men," this is how I described the poetry in the context of my field experience:

I was not in the habit of interviewing men. It was only after I returned home that I recognized how rich, moving, and disturbing my conversations with men had been; I also realized that part of their richness arose because I didn't have my research questions ready at hand. Men simply told me stories over a coffee or a beer, gifted me with their opinions and ideas and feelings without me having to ask them anything at all. In the end, it seemed more appropriate to reflect their stories in poetry so that I could record both sides of the conversations: the words that were spoken, and how they were received . . . Grappling with political and historical phenomenon of nationalism as an academic sometimes lead me to collapse the feelings of individuals into the actions of their political leaders. The conversations I had with veterans, in particular, reminded me, chided me, sometimes even shamed me into remembering the idiosyncratic nature of personal experience. This became more true, not less, when the subject at hand was violence, grief, and war. (Pintar 2010)

The men I spoke to in Croatia (not all ethnically Croatian) shared their lives as soldiers, as musicians, as sailors, as scholars, as friends, as fathers, and as sons. The lives and experiences of the soldiers I met were surprisingly different from one another. Some of the men were soldiers by profession, some had volunteered, and many had been conscripted. They all had been changed by their experiences, but their core identities for the most part remained what they had been before the war: they were still musicians, still scholars, still their mothers' sons. Those who had been disabled in the war struggled to figure out what they could be now, but I found them astonishingly without bitterness:

He came from Sarajevo
  to get a new leg since
  Serbs shot off the old one
  he doesn't like Zagreb
  too many Croatians
I miss Muslims, he says
  can you believe it
  I miss Serbs

After the publication of my poetry, I gave a public reading and recognized that not only could the stories recorded in my *other* notebooks be expressed poetically, but that they also had untapped pedagogical power. My second epiphany, which followed from the poetry reading, was that my field experiences, including those expressed as poetry, could be shared as *stories*.

THE SECOND EPIPHANY

I have taught from my *other* notebooks in many different classroom contexts, including general education courses addressing the nations of the former Yugoslavia, and Central and Eastern Europe, as well as in seminars addressing culture, identity, and diaspora more broadly. The challenge of teaching undergraduate students at the University of Illinois about the histories and cultures of the South Slavic nations, is that we draw large numbers of heritage students from the Chicago area. In the early 2000s, many of these students were former refugees. Some arrived in class knowing very little about their family and cultural history, and some came in with firmly held convictions about the war, its history, causes, victims, and villains. These beliefs were often, understandably, biased toward their own community's point of view and contradicted other students' equally firm convictions. I had to provide these students with a meta-position on their own histories, as well as teaching them from the syllabus. For students who were there to fulfill general education requirements and had no prior knowledge of the region (which they could not find on a map, but that's a different problem), I had the challenge of talking through a tangled historical record of violence without facilitating the emergence of the very stereotypes I was trying to avoid.

My *other* notebooks gave me a wealth of material from which to pull stories that allowed me to hammer away at a variety of mistaken ideas: that war comes about because people hate each other; that a nation can defined by its most extreme views; or that the characters of individuals can be judged by the actions of their authoritarian leaders. Everyone knows that "Croatians and Serbs hate each other," for example, and that this productively explains something. Stereotypically, it explains everything. To push back against what students heard growing up (and what they found on the Internet), I told stories from my field experiences in Croatia, walking them through my search to understand the Croatian experience of war, how people acted in the war, and the effect of the war on them. I also shared stories from my *other* notebooks, including the conversations that I had had with Serbs, Slovenes, Bosnians, Montenegrins, and Macedonians in my various travels, regarding their views and experiences of the region's recent conflicts and wars.

Among topics covered in these courses, I taught the siege of Dubrovnik, which lasted from October 1991 until June 1992. Civilians in the Croatian city of Dubrovnik were shelled in their homes by the Yugoslav army, under the control of Serbia, and in coordination with Montenegro, which occupied the hills above the city. During the year-long siege, people died, cultural heritage was destroyed, and the city's citizens suffered the effects of terror, which lingered after the conflict ended. To support the telling of these stories I sometimes read my poetry in class:

It's the nights that always come
   into my mind, he says
   all our relations crammed
   into one tiny house
   the children packed in a row
   on the living room floor
   if one turned over
   the rest had no choice but to turn
It was hard for me to sleep too, he says
   knowing if a shell hit the house
   if it hit the children
   there was no place I could take them
   and no one would come

He can't finish the story
he turns his head
he lights a cigarette

I also wanted to share with my students the fact that war certainly can make people feel hatred, but that it isn't a hatred they were born with; it is, rather, part of the calamity that befalls them. Hatred resulting from violence can be understood as post-traumatic, meaning that it represents an open, lingering wound. While I was in the field these wounds were active, just as the ancient stonework of the world heritage city was still being reconstructed. What I learned from people who had lived through it was that hatred didn't explain the war; it arose as collateral damage of the war, a tragedy in its own right:

In a wine shop
early in the morning
the old men gather around me
one presses a glass in my hand,
one shares a bite of salty fish
one places bread in my mouth
like a sacrament
he tells me how for twenty years
he lived in New York
making money for Yugoslav Air
I came home when the war began, he says
I can't tell you what it was like
shells falling, houses burning
boats in the harbor, burning
Serbs were my friends
all my life
now I hate them
he shakes his head at the wonder of it
I hate them

My field stories allowed me to explore more deeply with my students the Croatian experience, and to approach it from all sides, including the fact that Croatian nationalism in its extreme forms had become xenophobic, unwelcoming, and sometimes violent in its treatment of people who not long before had been fellow Yugoslav citizens. When I was in the field many people attested to this change. I spoke to a young Macedonian in Zagreb who was being deported from the country, and received from him the insight that hatred defines the hater, more than it has anything meaningful to do with what is hated:

He came from Macedonia,
   just finished his veterinary degree
   after eight years in Zagreb they give him
   three days to get out
   I wonder if he's angry
He says
   I pity them, really
   I don't have to hate anyone
   to be who I am
   my country is poor
   there's a doctor for every cow
   but so what? I own my own house
   and vegetables are cheap

In Croatia in the 1990s, I found wounds and trauma; I found intolerance, prejudice, and inane conspiracy theories; I also discovered that many Croatians, even under conditions of surging nationalism and war, had been able to hang on to their humanity and the prewar truths of their lives:

While he was fighting Serbs on the front lines
   his wife was hiding a Serb in their home
He wants me to understand:
   that's not what Croatian history will say
   but that's how it was.

Unfailingly, when I read these poems in the classroom (providing backstories and additional context) students would stop looking at their laptops and phones and really listen to what I was saying. When telling non-poetic field stories as well, I found that my students always asked more questions, and engaged with the issues more deeply than they did when we had discussions that covered similar ground even when based on excellent and compelling readings.

Though I didn't live through the war, and couldn't give personal witness to it, the fact that I went to the region there to see for myself what had happened, seemed to hold weight for my students. Because I personally knew Muslims who had been forced out of their homes by Serbs, and Croats who had been forced out of their homes by Muslims, and Serbs who had been forced out of their homes by Croats, I could attest to the fact that there was no side in the wars that attended the dissolution of Yugoslavia that did not suffer. The most important truth I tried to impart to my students is that acknowledging a group's suffering in the war, doesn't absolve their responsibility for crimes they committed (in this, or previous wars); likewise, judging one nation to be "more responsible" for war crimes in a particular place or time, doesn't negate the suffering of individuals in that group in other places and times. I have made that argument in academic writing, but in the classroom, storytelling in addition to discussion of films made in the region, seems to be the best combination for success in communicating it to students (Pintar 2020).

The sorts of reactions to war and violence that I observed in the field were not unique to the Croatian experience, of course, and there are poems in my *other* notebooks that speak to the wider human condition, which I have shared in a variety of courses. Croatians often told me how the war had changed their communities and relationships, making them less trusting, less caring, less generous. The following poem has successfully generated students' self-reflection on the link between trauma and trust within their own cultures, communities, and families:

Yesterday you gave your breath to a man
  where others stood, watching him die
  before the war, you say, they would not
  have been so afraid to touch a stranger
You didn't know him, but you could see
  he was someone's husband, someone's father
  and so you did what could be done
  though it was not enough
My friend, there could be no better prayer than this,
  to give him up to death
  because of you, the last experience of his life
  would not have to be a final bitter wound of war
Because of you, because of you,
  the last experience of his life
  could be a kiss

Philosophical, moral, and legal abstractions can be difficult to get general educational students to care enough about to grapple with. Storytelling as a classroom presentation style seems to be effective in breaking through that disinterest and freeing students to connect at deeper levels.

At the graduate level, I regularly presented on qualitative methodology to students engaged in Russian and East European and Eurasian studies. Graduate students are never disinterested when the topic is fieldwork. They seem to particularly value stories about stupid mistakes; these are pedagogically rich, since failure in the field is such an excellent teacher. There was that time, for example, that I was riding the overnight bus from Rovinj at the northern end of the Adriatic coast back down to the south. A man wearing combat fatigues, sitting at the back of the bus howled like a wolf intermittently all night long. No one could sleep, but no one objected. I couldn't understand why the bus driver didn't say something, why nobody turns around to look, why no one complained. I tried to ignore it, I tried to sleep, I even tried to write about it, but I was exhausted and irritated and at some point, I had had enough. In what I identified, even at the time, as an "ugly American" impulse to deal indignantly with the nightmarish situation myself, I started to turn around.

I honestly don't remember what I intended to do, whether to say something, get a better look at him, or just give him a steely stare, but the woman sitting next to me grabbed my arm to stop me. We had passed a few small pleasantries when we took our seats, and she knew I was a foreigner. She hissed at me to sit still. I whispered back to her my confusion. Why wouldn't the driver do something? There were old people and children on the bus. People needed to sleep.

She shrugged, a physical gesture I had come to understand as an indication of passive acceptance of (though not acquiescence to), unacceptable situations. She told me, what seems so obvious in retrospect, that the driver was frightened.

"He drives this bus every night. He's easy to find," she whispered. "If he kicks that guy off tonight, tomorrow the guy comes back and beats him." And then, as if maybe she thought the American woman was a complete idiot, she added. "Some people are crazy, you know, because of the war."

I thanked her and sat still as she told me to do, chastened and also relieved that I hadn't shown the guy my face. This story always engenders classroom discussion because it illustrates the vulnerability researchers have in the field before we fully understand the language. It also illuminates the strange cultural space we occupy that results from what we expect ourselves to do in the field which is to talk to people, talk to anyone really, often without a full understanding of conversational norms, social codes, and acceptable local behavior. In graduate-level seminars, when qualitative methods were discussed, I often shared with students the kinds of stories that provided answers to questions I wished I had asked before I went to the field. What is it like to live for a long period of time in a country that is not your own? What is it like to stick out, to feel awkward and misunderstood a lot of the time? And for the female students, how bad is the unwanted sexual attention, and how do you deal with it?

I warned students against the habit of nodding their heads when they're learning a language, still translating what they hear word for word, so as not to find themselves, as I did once, saying *da, da, da, yes, yes, yes,* to a man who was telling me in the middle of a public street how much he wanted to sleep with me. The entire time it took for the meaning of his words to take their slow trek from my ear to my brain, I had been nodding and repeating my stupid *da, da, da*. There was nothing I could do when I finally understood his meaning but turn heel and walk away. I have told this story many times. I tell it for the laugh so that students remember it and avoid making that kind of mistake themselves.

I had no idea when I packed to go to Croatia without my husband that there was a name for what I would be, socially, when I got there. I was a "white widow," a traditional term used for Dalmatian women whose husbands are alive, but out at sea. They are presumed to be sexually available, and are considered desirable partners, since they are unlikely to make emotional demands, given their need for secrecy. I was unprepared for the experience of being constantly hit on by strangers, or the presumption that I welcomed the attention. Had I known in graduate school the likelihood that I would be sexually harassed, or worse, maybe I wouldn't have been so paralyzed when I was physically assaulted in daylight by a middle-aged grocer who leaned over a cheese counter, to reach inside my blouse to pinch my breast. I was so stunned, I probably thanked him for the chunk of cheese he calmly wrapped for me before I took it to the cashier to pay. I couldn't tell the management what had happened; he *was* the management.

In my *other* notebooks, I recorded this story in fury, just as I wrote about all the other challenges of the field: confusion, awkwardness, frustration, disgust, culture shock, and homesickness. In rereading what I had to say about all of that, I can see that I was engaged in spontaneous but intensive self-therapy. By writing my experiences down I gained power over them. If I took the next step to turn them into poetry, I was able to gain something from even the most disturbing conversations (which I felt compelled to have, wanting to learn from everyone I met), rather than feeling that something had been taken away from me. I became a master of therapeutic mythologizing. The power, I discovered, was all in the frame.

I sit next to an aging Dalmatian sailor
   (his eyes are Adriatic blue)
   he is traveling to Paris to meet his married lover
   he enjoys her betrayal of her husband and scoffs
   when I attest my own fidelity
I smell the truth on your skin, he says
   and strokes with his tanned finger
   my bare arm
   you were so close to giving in, and
   next time you will
I have to laugh (from sheer relief) to know
   the devil can make such a mistake
   about the nature of desire

We go into the field with a presumption of benevolence from the people we meet. Far and away, most people I met, men and women, old and young, were kind as well as generous with their time and their stories. But it's unwise to assume everyone will be. Field stories can powerfully communicate to graduate students that they need to consider their own need for self-care and safety, just as they plan to protect their research subjects. Exploring ways of writing in the field in modes *other than* expected standard academic prose, can be an aspect of that care.

THE THIRD EPIPHANY

A few years after completing my PhD, I returned to Croatia. One of the young women who had been involved in the participatory research, who had afterward become a close friend, asked me if I had ever finished my novel.

"Novel?" I clearly remember my surprise at that. "Is that what you thought I was writing?" She remembered then that I had been doing some kind of sociological research. But did I write a book about them, she wanted to know. I told her that unfortunately, I had not.

"Good," she immediately replied. "Because if you did, we would hate you now."

That was a gut punch but not a real surprise. "Why?" I asked, bracing myself for condemnation. What she said next provided me with a moment of extraordinary clarity in the long arc story of my life.

"Well," she said, flicking her ashes, and shifting her vocal tone to what I referred to in my *other* notebooks as *scary Croatian woman voice*, "How can you understand anything? You didn't live through the war. You weren't here. What right do you have to analyze us and our suffering?" She checked my expression, to see how hard this was landing, and then softened her face and her voice. "But you chose to live with us for what, one-two years? You sat right next to us all through that dark, depressing time. We have to admit, you probably have insights."

The conversation then moved on to other things, but what stayed with me was the contrast between her cheerfulness when she asked if I had finished my novel, and her flashing anger when she thought about me writing an academic book, using an "expert" voice to analyze their experiences. That conversation marked the real end of an ethnography based on my dissertation. *But—a novel?* No, surely not. However, there was a reason for my friend's misremembering. As it happened, one boring, smoke-filled evening, while I was in the field, I pitched a murder story, asking the random friends, acquaintances and strangers in the café bar where I was a regular, to describe the suspects and their motives. They gave me a lot of ideas that night, which of course I wrote down in my *other* notebook.

It took me several more years to actually give novel writing a try, and before I did, I had to travel back to Croatia to ask the people who were to be the principle influences on the characters for permission to fictionalize some of their words and experiences—and to ask them what they wanted their character names to be. The writing of the first draft of the novel finally occurred in a flood: in three months, I had produced 150,000 words of long-dammed up thoughts, stories, and the insights my friend granted I probably had.

The first version of the novel barely concealed my dissertation. It lifted countless details from my *other* notebooks. It told the story of a writer who came to Dubrovnik to write a mystery novel; which she based on the people she met, and the conversations that she had, which in turn were based on mine.

> It began as technique, settled into habit, and was now a daily compulsion. Lily's first pass through the world was careless, wordless. She gazed with imperfect eyes. Then she noticed what Rachel would see: details, inconsistencies, absences. Inside one of Lily's novels Rachel would call them clues, but in her own life they were only the mundane byproducts of her second, unnatural way of seeing.

I see in my depiction of Lily and her novelist character Rachel, a representation of my own bifurcated field experience. It is fair to say that I walked through the world using two different sets of eyes, one careless and imperfect, and the other academic and unnatural. My two sets of notebooks and the kinds of writing that came from each, offer clear testimony to the differences.

On the advice of a literary agent, I chopped the novel in half, losing most of the theoretical discussions of trauma that happened between the characters—my research inexpertly concealed in dialogue. The agent who reviewed the next version told me there was not enough action. It came to me then, that perhaps what I needed to do was to write the novel that the novelist was writing, since that's where all the action was. It took me a few more years, but I did write Rachel's historical mystery, which in turn evolved into magical realism. I gave agency to saints and angels who have been credited with saving the city over its 1,500-year history. A complicated entanglement of storylines explore not just trauma, but resilience.

The first agent to weigh in on that version told me it was unpublishable: "too many stories," she said. The thing may never see print. But recently, my professional life has shifted again, and I find myself teaching game design. From this new vantage, it has occurred to me that the complex and multistranded storytelling that the last agent objected to, may lend itself to an interactive digital format. As a work of electronic literature, it would allow readers to get beneath the surface of Rachel's novel to find Lily, its author. Maybe I could allow the reader to go deeper still and find the social and cultural analysis of trauma that I removed. And maybe under that, they might find the ethnographer too, completely banished because I had been so careful to erase myself from the frame. Twenty years later, perhaps it is time to put myself back.

The idea that poetics could serve qualitative data analysis is in its third decade of consideration and application (Denzin 1996, 2019). Poetic, experimental and arts-based methodologies, often in coordination with participatory research are being practiced, albeit still at the margins, but across many different qualitative disciplines (Boudreault-Fournier 2020; Norris et al. 2020; Hanauer 2015; Maynard and Cahnmann-Taylor 2010). Arguably, many of the things that we learn in the field, including factual events and even quantifiable data may be *better* expressed through stories beautifully told, than in academic prose, with its narrow range of uninspiring and often obscure rhetorical styles. Which expression better captures life as it is lived, and as an ethnographer observes it in the field? In the context of teaching, which better communicates cultural experiences to students? In my experience it has been my storytelling, my gameful role-playing activities, my poetry, and my fiction, rather than my academic writings, that have served my students best.

Other than a couple of poems, including what I have shared here, I have published very few stories from my field research. That fact is irrelevant to their pedagogical power. Their main audience, and arguably, the most important one, has been students. My field experiences have been a gift that has provided inspiration for a dizzying array of transmedia storytelling—narratives traveling from casual conversations to journal notes, to poetry, to performance, to fiction, and next, perhaps to interactive digital narrative. Storytelling has allowed me to communicate what I learned about the former Yugoslavia, about Croatia, nationalism, war, and trauma, and to share this knowledge in multiple classroom contexts with powerful effect.

The difference between the divergent expressions of my field work experience reflects the difference between my two notebooks, my two ways of seeing. The poetics of encounter that I explored in my *other* notebooks embraced doubt, whimsy, and miracles, three notes I felt that I could not play in my dissertation and that, until now, do not appear anywhere in my academic writing. But I heard their music many times when I was in the field, informing what I learned, what I have to teach, and all the stories that I tell.

He will work three years of civil service
 instead of eight months in the military
 I love my country, he says

but I won't hate
and I won't learn how to kill
The neighborhood cat is back
  jumps into his lap again
  and drops something in my hand:
  her kitten, just newborn

We were victims in the war, he says
  victims of course, look around
  but Croatians also did terrible things
  he comforts the mother
  while I cradle the tiny life
  afraid to move or speak

REFERENCES

Abdela, Lesley. 2007. "'Anyone Here Been Raped and Speaks English?': Workshops for Editors and Journalists on Gender-Based Violence and Sex-Trafficking." *Gender & Development*, 15(3): 387–398.

Behr, Edward. 1985. *Anyone Here Been Raped and Speaks English?* Hachette: Hodder & Stoughton.

Boudreault-Fournier, Alexandrine. 2020. *Aerial Imagination in Cuba: Stories from above the Rooftops*. London: Routledge.

Boyden, Jo. 2004. "Anthropology under Fire: Ethics, Researchers and Children in War." In *Children and Youth on the Front Line: Ethnography, Armed Conflict and Displacement*, edited by Jo Boyden and Joanna de Berry, 237–258. Oxford, NY: Berghahn Books.

Burman, Michele J., Susan A. Batchelor, and Jane A. Brown. 2001. "Researching Girls and Violence. Facing the Dilemmas of Fieldwork." *British Journal of Criminology*, 41(3): 443–459.

Clark, Janine Natalya. 2012. "Fieldwork and Its Ethical Challenges: Reflections from Research in Bosnia." *Human Rights Quarterly*, 34: 823–839.

Cushman, Thomas. 2004. "Anthropology and Genocide in the Balkans: An analysis of Conceptual Practices of Power." *Anthropological Theory*, 4(1): 5–28.

Denzin, Norman K. 1996. *Interpretive Ethnography: Ethnographic Practices for the 21st Century*. Thousand Oaks, CA: Sage Publications.

Denzin, Norman K. 2019. "Answering the Call." *Qualitative Inquiry*, 25(6): 529–530.

Hanauer, David Ian. 2015. "Being in the Second Iraq War: A Poetic Ethnography." *Qualitative Inquiry*, 21(1): 83–106.

Huisman, Kimberly. 2008. "Does This Mean You're Not Going to Come Visit Me Anymore?': An inquiry into an Ethics of Reciprocity and Positionality in Feminist Ethnographic Research." *Sociological Inquiry*, 78(3): 372–396.

Kirkevold, Marit and Ådel Bergland. 2007. "The Quality of Qualitative Data: Issues to Consider when Interviewing Participants Who Have Difficulties Providing Detailed Accounts of their Experiences." *International Journal of Qualitative Studies on Health and Well-Being*, 2(2): 68–75.

Maynard, Kent and Melisa Cahnmann-Taylor. 2010. "Anthropology at the Edge of Words: Where Poetry and Ethnography Meet." *Anthropology and Humanism*, 35(1): 2–19.

Moyle, Wendy. 2002. "Unstructured Interviews: Challenges When Participants Have a Major Depressive Illness." *Journal of Advanced Nursing*, 39(3): 266–273.

Norris, Joe, Kakali Bhattacharya, and Kimberly Powell. 2020. "Embodying Moral Discourses through Arts-Based Methodologies: Poetry, Visual Arts, Movement, Sounds, and Performance." *Cultural Studies ↔ Critical Methodologies*, 20(1): 3–6.

Özerdem, Alpaslan, and Richard Bowd. 2016. Participatory research methodologies: Development and post-disaster/conflict reconstruction. Milton Park, Abingdon, Oxon: Routledge.

Pintar, Judith. 2000. "Anticipating Consequences: What Bosnia Taught Us about Healing the Wounds of War." *Human Rights Review*, 1(2): 56–66.

Pintar, Judith and Steven J. Lynn. 2008. *Hypnosis: A Brief History*. Oxford: Blackwell-Wiley.

Pintar, Judith. 2010. "Feminine Nouns that End in a Consonant: Conversations with Croatian Men." *Ulbandus XIII: The Wound and the Imagination*, 13: 139–146.

Pintar, Judith A. 2020. "The Problem of Innocence: Suicide in the films of Vinko Brešan, Goran Paskaljević, and Pjer Zalica." *Paper presented at the 52nd Association for Slavic, East European, and Eurasian Studies Annual Convention*, Washington, DC.

Stubbs, Paul and Baljit Soroya. 1996. "War Trauma, Psycho-Social Projects, and Social Development in Croatia." *Medicine, Conflict and Survival*, 12: 303–314.

Torbert, William R. 2000. "Transforming social science: Integrating quantitative, qualitative, and action research." In *Transforming Social Inquiry, Transforming Social action*, edited by Francine T. Sherman and William R. Torbert, 67–91. Springer, Boston, MA, 2000.

Chapter 3

Trained Identities

Exploring Emergent Identities aboard One Slow-Moving Train

William H. Leggett

INTRODUCTION

I[1] want to tell you about a cross-country trip I took as an anthropology gradu-ate student to San Francisco back in 1996.[2] This is a story I tell my students in an attempt to explain the various ways anthropological knowledge can be put to use in our everyday encounters. These notes take shape through an examination of casual interactions with strangers inside one slow-moving train car (Bhimull 2014; Syring and Offen 2017). What makes this field experience of cross-country travel worthy of investigation, I believe, is the unique context offered by way of rail. On a train, the usual social ties of place, of work, of family and home are largely circumvented by the meandering passage of cars traveling an iron highway through mountains, deserts, farms, towns, and the monotonous black of night. As rail passengers, as strangers on a train, we found connections not through family ties or regional affilia-tion, history or heritage. Whatever connections we found were created ad-hoc within the more immediate shared intimacy of time shared in a space of travel technology (Vannini 2011). Fabian makes the critical point that "for human communication to occur, coevalness has to be created" (1983: 30–31). Communication, in other words, is about sharing time as much as, if not more than, about sharing space. I think that whatever differences there might have been among us as passengers, we were able to, almost forced to, share an experience that was both contained in (the train car itself) and traveling through space (Westward). Movement, it turns out, takes time.

It is this cohabitation of time and space that sparked my interest in review-ing the interactions that make up the heart of this chapter. As rail travelers we existed—except those that worked aboard the train—outside our usual spheres of influence and interaction (Mortensen and Nicholas 2010). What I was able to observe and what I try to describe below are the verbal and kinetic interactions of social actors producing ourselves in a space free of the usual constraints of everyday life, operating in a time of its own rhythms, creating narratives that reveal, at least in part, the potentials and constraints of our own autobiographies.

On this journey, as with any journey, connections are made between ideas, between places and people, between memories and experiences that, while seemingly obvious at the time, lose some coherence in their retelling (Stoller 2007). I try here not to replace that lost coherence with some other, but instead ask the audience (previously, in the classroom, now as readers) to recognize the way thoughts wander and conversations sway and swerve like the rhythms of a moving train.

TRAVELING NARRATIVES

You board the train, a commuter, in Bloomington-Normal, one of many twin cities in the flatness of Illinois. It is Wednesday and you will not be in San Francisco until Friday. Your bags are heavy with books, booze, crackers, smoked sausage, shirts, underwear, and a couple of zip-locked sandwiches. The last of your bartending tips, a little less than a hundred in small bills, make your wallet fat and uncomfortable. But you sit on the leather lump and anxiously await the train's first jolt forward.

Then you are in Chicago transferring to a long string of cars, the *California Zephyr*, your home the rest of the way across the United States. You stuff your bag into the rack above your head and settle in for a long turns-out-to-be largely sleepless journey. The train jolts forward and a rhythm takes hold. Your body rocks side-to-side on a metal tide that takes you West.

The next three hours you stare at the backdoor landscape the rail-line offers of dark-dirt-tilled land disturbed now and again by a parallel-running back-road pock-marked here and there with a silo or a shed of rusted metal until the sun sets and all you see is your reflection. Then the lights pick up and a town comes into view and everything jolts to a stop to pick up and drop off people. Then eventually the cars lurch slowly back into darkness. Then the pattern repeats again and again with the times between spaced farther and farther apart.

Out the window you see Interstate 80 displaying the repetitive arc of street lights, the bare cement-blocked store-backs, bathrooms and dumpsters of *Dairy Queens*, *Dollar Stores*, *Walmarts*, and *Amoco's*. Past that you see the older road known as *Lincoln Highway*. In seemingly defiant response *Lincoln*

Highway has lined itself with the carcasses of campers and cars, end-of-times biblical billboards and fried-fish restaurants, wind-slanted corrugated buildings, and stacked up brake drums striped from rain and rust. These artifacts of our industrialized pasts appear to satirize time in their denial of the sanitized modernist landscape Interstate 80, with its toll booths and flyovers, has to offer. You are riding tracks twice removed from the daily commutes of early and mid-twentieth-century Midwestern America. You are on tracks twice removed from the present.

You are fortunate because academics handed you a legitimate purpose and destination for your juvenile travels. You are on your way to San Francisco, as a scholar of sorts, to attend the biggest event your discipline holds, the annual meeting of the American Anthropological Association.

Several hours some drinks and one Lawrence Grossberg paper later you find your way to the lounge car. It is a fluorescently lit display of blues and reds sun-faded and cigarette-burned. Two sisters from Atlanta possess the space. They are a gorgeous mess of black hair and red lips bundled up in denim and leather. They swagger and smirk and it quickly becomes clear they have been elected hosts of whatever festivities the lounge car has to offer. They stroll the aisle and mingle with ease, touching shoulders and mussing hair and laughing over the noise of the rails passing beneath your feet, assuming, rightly it turns out, we are all part of their rollicking party.

Eventually, their strolling and your sitting collide and these young white Atlanta sisters make their conversation your own. "New Mexico sucks. I would never live there. All that New Age bullshit, rubbing rocks while sitting on your ass. Jesus. No thanks." You nod, laugh, and smile. You all clunk plastic Solo cups and drink. The combination of corporeal signals marks your entry into the sisters' rambling state-by-state commentary and off you go.

"I spent some time in Texas," says the sister on the left. "Austin is a cool town. I had a great time. Didn't ever have to work. Did the bar-buffets every night. Nuts and cherries, oranges and olives and free drinks. I swear I never slept. Like for two weeks or something. Go to clubs. Just go to clubs. You know you can drive with alcohol in the car? Just open."

"There are these guys on the street," says the Atlanta sister on the right as she brushes cigarette embers from the breast of her leather jacket. "I swear to God, with suits and vests, and cowboy boots and cowboy hats, and those big loopy mustaches. And they've got guns! Strapped to their waists, *and* they've got briefcases . . . like they're going to some business meeting."[3]

"That wasn't Austin. That was Houston."

"We went to this guy's house to set up '*hors d'oeuvres*' and the bar for his party . . . his '*soiree*.' We drove for something like 45 minutes and he said, 'OK, we're here.' And I was looking and there was nothing. Nada! We had just turned into his driveway!"

You all laugh.

"It took another hour or something before we got to his house. Big. As. Fuck!"

The Atlanta sisters are on their way to California to find work in food services for the entertainment industry in Los Angeles and, at least for the meantime, to move in with their Dad. They have befriended JT, a young Black man who could maybe pass for eighteen if you squinted just right, and who you later learn is on his way to Arizona to join the CIA. JT wears loose and wide blue jeans hanging low, a hooded sweatshirt over his natural locks, and would rather not say where he is from (security reasons, he says). He sports a winter-weather black mask that covers the bottom of his nose, his mouth and chin. Next to JT, pressed into the crook between the seats and the carpeted wall below the window, sits Ed, a seventeen-year-old born-again Christian who professes a liking for vodka. His girlfriend, he says, waits for him in California with hopes of consummating their relationship. You all joke that her prospects strike you as slim.

Down in the back of the car sits a teen you recognize as little more than a guitar playing, Grateful Dead loving, blonde-locked, dope-smoking, Colorado-bound stereotype. Was there more there? You never gave him a chance. In other corners sit silent sleepless individuals staring at what cannot be seen through the windows or in themselves. And there you are content staring at your own blurry reflection in the blackness of a nighttime window. The constant clatter and doubled-thump of car wheels over rail connectors rattle their way into silence—the kind of noise you do not notice until it has disappeared. What time is it?

In the lounge car you feel a spy of individuals—your fellow travelers—in the act of invention. Having been on the train longer than you they have found a transient fidelity in their constant returns to the traveling bar. You are simply a new recruit. Welcome to the club; membership is free but if you share your bottle initiation is quicker. Alcohol brings freedom to a conversation already liberated through each passenger's knowledge of inevitable departure . . . and separation. Calculation and hesitance—the weighing of thoughts—are unnecessary and unwelcome deterrents to open debate and rambling oration. You sit and drink and listen.

Without markers, without relations and without allegiances, the passengers present experiences in the construction of themselves (and yourself); trying to put some weight to the shapes and voices filling the void of the train. Mary Steedly writes, "The transfer and transcription of historical experience . . . is the movement through which subjectivity is produced" (1993: 22). Yet, in your moving state, what chance is there to question what holds your stories in, connects you to your pasts? Your pasts, it seems, are somehow free to roam aboard the train. There is no second-guessing, no correcting or clarifying taking place in your conversations (save for the familial banter between the Atlanta sisters). You are just talking.

How do people construct themselves in a space separate from place in a time without consequence? On the train you have all found your spots—temporary as they may be—within a moving, dislocated machine. But these are the awkward positions of individuals separate from the usual relations through which life experiences reverberate. These autobiographical echoes are usually essential in reminding you who you are and who you have been. Through your relations, you are constructed as you come, fitfully to be sure, to occupy social positions prescribed by your relations and the institutions within which you find yourselves. You experiment with subjectivities that are, nonetheless constrained through the telling and retelling, affirming and denying, of your experiences. It is a complicated process.

But now, on this train, must your tales be true? Do you have to replicate information through which you identify (or are identified) in other social contexts? Who is going to check, validate, correct? There is no presumption in your lounge car of reuniting later to "catch-up" with each other's lives. There is no second-guessing. You are just talking.

NARRATING RACE AND GENDER

Somewhere within the train, or through the windows, or in your memory something brews: a historical concoction of personal experience, movies seen and books read, stories and snippets of sound and music, jokes you thought you knew but didn't really, faces yelling and staring and ordering food and drink and failing to hide emotions, comic images with real voices and years and years of anthropological texts.

You think now of all those texts; anthropologist after anthropologist sticking his head through the overgrowth; entering while discursively creating the frontier. What ambitions were they fulfilling? What was it to be an explorer and an intellectual in the age of colonial encounter? The land now split by the rail, is this the frontier? Nostalgia perhaps, or guilt, or bourbon wallows within you, challenging the innocence of the journey. This is just traveling. Nothing more. No need to bring anthropology's baggage along. You have packed enough.

"Ed, go sit your sorry ass down. What kind of name is Ed anyway? Ed. Shit. Ed. Ed. Egh. Engh. Eh." His name is played with by JT until it turns into little more than an egg without end. Ed exits the conversation by putting on his headphones. Can he hear? The need for sleep pushes one of the Atlanta sisters out the door. Her recently acquired "train legs" fight a less than epic battle with the vodka and bourbon in her body as she bounces about in a counterpoint to the rhythm of the train. You and JT watch with curiosity. The door slides open, a metallic racket intrudes momentarily, and she disappears, with a sharp steel finale, to a car full of those insistent on the illusion of sleep. Turning to the remaining Atlanta sister JT begins, "Girl I don't know why you think black people are any more racist than white."

"Cause I grew up in Atlanta, ok?! I lived there and was discriminated against. That city is something like 70 percent Black and I know what it's like to be in the minority. So don't talk to me about racism, alright? Cause I've experienced it. People stare at you. Give you looks, you know?!"

Atlanta sister is a traveler with connections to the live music world. She has, she says, worked in bars and clubs in New York, LA, Atlanta and other metropolises. She can talk about Chicago, New Orleans, Miami all from experience. As she speaks you note the interconnections of experience and authority in the creation of a reality that cannot be questioned. You note the use of statistics (70%?), seemingly imaginary in your eyes, to prop up her arguments. You note the authoritative power of numbers, if not for the audience, at least for the speaker.

"People always stare at you and treat you like you don't belong. I've been told to move cause it's a Black neighborhood. You know, sometimes you don't get your food cause you're White. I know it's because I'm White. Forget it."

Atlanta sister's discrimination story is full of openings; opportunities for some other in the group to proclaim a similar experience. She stares at you while she speaks. "Yeah," I think, you are supposed to say, with an enthusiastic nod of understanding. But you do not. No one does. And the quiet sits. And it lingers. And these unfilled gaps of affirmation bring the story to a halt.

The silence is too long. No one picks up the thread. No one contradicts the argument. And you drift from the narrative searching for something better to talk about. But Atlanta sister returns to tales of travel and music. Her past run-ins with racism mingle almost randomly with stories of a life spent in nightclubs hanging out with the cutting edge of America's punk and industrial music scenes. She assures you she knows the right people, performers, and places in the right cities.

Each place is linked to an experience. Each experience is part of who she is. These experiences are used to create a certain kind of cosmopolitan authority. She was there. She lived it. She knows. You cannot help but think of Baudrillard's contempt for realists.

It has to be said that the propagandists of reality vent that contempt on themselves first of all, reducing their own lives to an accumulation of facts and evidence, causes and effects. Well-ordered resentment always begins at home. (1996: 95)

But something is not working on the audience. Atlanta sister's experiences are lacking in depth. Her story set in Atlanta sounds a lot like the experience she had in Los Angeles. Both remind you of the week she didn't sleep in Chicago. You are constantly shown the inside of a club; the graffitied walls, the skanky bathrooms, the hot bartenders, and a crowd of people all in on the secret. The bands change, though, and this is your clue to a new place, a new experience. It is a personal history without specificity. And it is a history that goes mostly unchallenged by the audience. By you.

"Little Five Points is a blast. The Olympics ruined it but before it was great.[4] We were left alone and the bands would stay, you know, around there. And you could party all night without any shit. Have you been there? The best shows! Me and my sister worked down there and hung out with, you know, all the punks from California and New York. All the goths . . . Siouxsie, The Cure, . . . um . . . ." Her thought sits unfinished.

This is local play, identity construction with the assistance of a vacant past. Individuals are constantly making and unmaking their worlds. Atlanta girl is a rocker. JT is a spy. Ed is a Born-Again Christian. You are a graduate student. Lyotard writes that the current age is concerned only with local issues, not with history but with problems to be solved, not with a grand reality but with games (1984). Are you all playing games? Trying out social roles like actors in some poorly-plotted uneventful Agatha Christie story? You wonder what allegiance Atlanta sister has to the identity she has created. Is all life this hollow when repeated? Her experiences, assembled it seems on the spot from the bits and pieces lying within her memory, stand before you now unchallenged by the slightest verbal note of discontent. Jameson writes that history, when constructed as a list,

> is not a list of facts or historical realities (although its items are not invented and are in some sense "authentic"), but rather a list of stereotypes, of ideas of facts and historical realities. (Jameson 1991: 279)

The past is supposed to come to life through Atlanta sister's stories of landmarks erased of little but alcohol and music. Train turns to time machine as she flashes back. But Atlanta sister has not brought you along for the ride. Her travels do not mean anything to her audience. Why not? Where did you get left behind? Then your own journey comes back to you and you realize at that moment even "male bonding" on a train has a legacy. The American novel, as Said has pointed out, is full of male adventure that combines travel with drama and aspiration.

> There is . . . a cultural motif long associated with picaresque tales in which a male adventurer . . . and his male companions are engaged in the pursuit of a

special dream—like Jason, Odysseus, or, even more compellingly, Don Quixote with Sancho Panza. In the field or on the open road, two men can travel together more easily, and they can come to each other's rescue more credibly than if a woman were along. So the long tradition of adventure stories, from Odysseus and his crew to the Lone Ranger and Tonto, Holmes and Watson, Batman and Robin, seems to hold. (Said 1993: 138)

But you grasp for no special dream just a break from reality. And you find no consolation in the idea that this traveling fiction is much more Hope and Crosby, *Road to Morocco* than Zane Grey, *Riders of the Purple Sage*, and is nowhere close to Jack Kerouac's *On The Road*. You no longer buy into a false premise of a frontier constructed in the colonial mind of a former America and consolidated in a literature that first naturalized and later brought to consciousness the ideas behind the practices of empire building. There is a history and an education you cannot escape, even on a train.

Colorado-bound stereotype offers you his guitar. You hold it and try to play but it does not resonate. Chords sound warped and the strings bend uncontrollable under the weight of your fingers. Why can't you tune the thing? Maybe it's the guitar. Maybe it can only play songs by Grateful Dead and Neil Young. Something is wrong with your fingers. They seem too big for your hand. Why can't you hear? It is too late and the instrument is not your friend. Slowly and then more quickly the lights of a small brick building approach then linger briefly beside the train. Your image stutters in and out of view as your reflection flickers and bounces against street lamps that fade back and away. It is dark again. You reach once more for the *George Dickel*.

As many have noted before, the past is constantly structured and restructured as an essential tool for the creation of a present. What has been less noted is how sometimes we misunderstand the present and, therefore, construct an unacceptable or at least unpalatable past. Narrative's schizophrenic position between "history as production" and "history as representation" opens the door for such a misapplication of experience. And this is what Atlanta sister has done. Prompted by a long loosely-connected conversation that preceded your presence, Atlanta sister spoke of her past in terms of race, and carried the categories over into the present situation, a social context it turns out she did not fully understand or control. In an attempt to divide her audience along color lines, Atlanta sister lost her hold on the audience.

Body language: folded arms, crossed legs, a slouching spine and distant eyes and the subsequent silence tell you there is an ill fit between the storied-identity Atlanta sister wishes to present and the reaction of her lounge mates. The long silent spaces that puncture her monologue on racial experiences make clear this was *not* a tale open to everybody (but one) as she first thought.

People always stare at you and treat you like you don't belong. I've been told to move cause it's a Black neighborhood. You know, sometimes you don't get your food cause you're White. I know it's because I'm White. Forget it.

Jonathan Friedman writes that making history is a way of producing identity "insofar as it produces a relation between what has supposedly occurred in the past and the present state of affairs" (1994: 118). But perhaps the present state of affairs was not quite as Atlanta sister thought.

As conversation begins again and topics move along trivial lines you—through laughter and nods of agreement—show an alliance with JT that perhaps forces Atlanta sister to reassess her audience, if not the position she has created for herself through storytelling. You conclude her narrative lacks what Said would call the "authority of the community" (1993).

Minutes pass. The train does not move. You all stare at the same backside of the same building that has been staring at you for the last half hour. The silence on the train is now but a continuation of the empty-seeming world outside. You are comfortable in the quiet. You always have been. Sometimes you enjoy the game of waiting out other people's discomfort. Where in time is the breaking point. Who will be the first to utter an innocuous phrase? You are thinking about a dinner party at a professor's house and your attempts at humor that fell flat when you see JT stir a bit. He has not been contemplating the silence.

While making use of the unspoken connection between race and violence, JT adroitly skirts Atlanta sister's line of argument and instead, sparked by a long past comment, turns to the generalized topic of murder: murder as a racial style, a cultural practice:

> Well, you know we just kill ourselves over a Welfare check or something while you all do that freaky shit when you kill. Whenever I hear about some crazy ass with a head in his freezer I know it's a White guy. You never hear about one of us going into a McDonald's and opening up on a crowd of strangers. It's always the White guy who is gonna save the body parts, keep the ass in the freezer.

The tone and rhythm are of stand-up comedy. The routine, maybe his own, maybe a bit of media consumption, mark a shift in storyteller and tale. The Atlanta sister leaves without saying good-bye. You do not see her again.

Through his stories, JT moves you back to the silence that was left open after the Atlanta sister's discrimination tale.

"I walk down the train and everybody looks up at me like I'm gonna steal their shit. Just cause I'm Black and the way I dress and my mask. Shit, my Versace underwear costs more than all their shit. Why would I want their sorry ass shit?"

"How much does your underwear cost?"

"One hundred dollars."

"You've got to be fucking kidding."

"Shit no. I tell you. It's worth it. When a lady sees my Versace's, I'm telling you, it's worth it.

You laugh.

"Nobody asks me what I'm up to. I been on this train for two days and nobody gives a shit where I'm going."

"Where are you going JT?"

"Shit."

"Where are you going?"

"I'm going to Arizona to join the CIA."

JT and you share a look of disbelief you read as a knowing wink. Too much information. Time to sleep.

FIRST PERSON REFLECTIONS

After the fact, there was clearly a lot going on during this interaction. At the time I was, if I am to be kind to myself, impervious to the identity politics being played out throughout this encounter. JT was clearly aware of the racial component of our group and our conversation. And the Atlanta sister was, in hindsight, clearly frustrated with our male bonding in relation to her performed narrative. Maybe the ignorance I might have claimed to the identity play before me, if called to the carpet, was coded into my very being from the earliest days of life as a white male.

The race-based discourse was explicit enough. It was spoken in the words of at least two in our party. But the gendered aspects of our conversation were less clear, at least at the time. Gendered words were not used. There was no discussion of discrimination based on being female. It was, I think, the unmarked presence of gender in our male-centered dismissal of the Atlanta sister's attempts to connect that deserves some reflection. Race was explicit in our words. But gender was there just as powerfully, lurking in our bodies, dividing us through a tacit male silence and stillness.

There was, it turns out, a debate taking place that put race and gender in a head-to-head match. How often does it happen that race and gender are evoked almost simultaneously, only to find that they are the dividing and uniting lines around which a discussion builds upon itself? If gender is unspoken, does it mean that the rules for gendered debate are as well? Does it mean that the field is already slanted against a fair airing of the issues of gendered discrimination that a woman encounters on a daily basis?

What if I or others had engaged in Atlanta sister's stories? What if we all had helped her by asking questions, by added anecdotes of our own, fleshed out the narratives she told through tales of our own experiences? Our contributions would not have to be racial (though the racial nature of her stories did play a role in at least my own hesitance). Our contributions could have hit on any number of points: clubs, music, work, places. What if we had found common ground (Turner 2008; Tanaka 2009)? What if we had not sat silent with folded arms? What if we had learned their names?

IS THIS FIELDWORK?

Because experiences do not necessarily move logically forward in the way of a mystery novel or a one-hour crime drama, they are by nature haphazard and, more often than not, contradictory. When we retell our experiences, we are therefore often selective in our narrative choices. We want things to make sense. And, at times, we might be rather superficial. This superficiality could be read as something of a fishing expedition—an opening or a search for connections, community, and social context. But in this superficiality, we often draw on what might be called "essentialist" categories of identification (Somers 1994: 605). Our reliance on such categories, particularly in the identification of others, should not lead one to conclude that our identities are fixed. While these are certainly powerful identifying markers, they are, as JT demonstrates, malleable; capable of becoming creative components in narratives of self-making.

Kathleen Stewart, in her remarkable book, *A Space on the Side of the Road* (1996), describes the act of social placement this way:

> People who meet must *place* each other, sifting through signs of identity that drift off into drama and mysterious connection in the narrative logic of contingency, engagement, encounter, and revelation. Social place becomes a sign not of a fixed social order but of the social imaginary immanent in *ways.* (1996: 201)

The placement process is an active search for identifications. The identifications narrated above were simultaneously inclusive and exclusive. The train car became a space where multiple registers ricocheted off the walls as the lived context of identity production. Through stories, JT was positioned as both a Man and as a Black Man—in the process shifting from social actor to social object. Atlanta sister was both White Woman and Woman. As such she too was made an object. But that is not the end of the story. Paying attention to voices, as Stewart has done, we are able to see how identifying categories were creatively deployed and how they were accepted (or not) through speech acts, silence, and body language.

In her writing, Stewart avoids a problem many of us encounter when we use identity categories to help us locate the individuals that occupy our ethnographies. She does not conflate identity with the fixed categories of race, class, gender, and so on, but, instead, allows the voices she encountered in space to express the staccato processes of identification through which these markers are evoked, challenged, appropriated, and through the act of appropriation, redefined.

The argument for a narrative approach to identity production within the social sciences is often framed in terms of narrative's ability to disrupt the power of essentialist categories such as race, class, and gender (Abelmann 1997; Somers 1994; Rorty 1976; Battaglia 1995; Bruner 1986). Others have argued against the ascendancy of narrative analysis in the social sciences, claiming that a focus on identities emergent through narrative discounts the reality of lived experience within the constitutive frames of a shared culture or history (Beatty 2010; Rosaldo 1980; Schweder 1991). However, taking narratives as creative productions does not deny the existence of social, political, and cultural constraints upon identity production (Bourgois 2003). Limitations exist not just because of the asymmetrical positions of power within which social persons must negotiate their subjectivity, but also because of the acceptable norms and prescribed desires of the speech community within which the individual is positioned. The narratives I witnessed onboard the train were simultaneously speaking creatively to the local context in which they were produced and to "wider negotiations of meaning and power" (Tsing 1993: 9). In this regard, race and gender were particularly relevant without being essentialist.

Vannini writes that "in wishing to do away with the repetitions, the structure, the orders, the givens, and the identities of representation," nonrepresentational ethnographies seek to "give us a sense of the ephemeral, the fleeting, and the not-quite graspable" (2015: 6). Avoiding a deep-dive into the history, strengths, and weaknesses of nonrepresentational theory, let me just say that I have tried to capture something of the emergent process through which placement of self and other is negotiated in everyday encounters. I've tried to show, through storytelling, the fleeting nature of alliances built and dismantled; the ways our bodies reveal attachment and ambivalence; the ways identity markers land on bodies, get brushed aside, then linger long after the words have passed. At the same time, we were just talking.

Let me conclude by pointing out that train travel in the late 1990s was an analog experience in a digital age. There is a pace to rail travel that allows connections to be made that might not be if traveling at different speeds within differently configured spaces. There is an analogy to be made between train travel and ethnography; the tempo of connection and analysis. Storytelling takes time. As does observation. The experiences of the Atlanta sisters, JT, and myself were at a pace observable enough to allow reflection. And they were close enough together in time and space for the casual observer to draw relevant connections. This kind of casual observation might lie at the edge of ethnography but, I would contend, proceeds at an ethnographic tempo and within an ethnographic space—shared, leisurely, and temporary—increasingly rare in American society (Stewart 2017).

NOTES

1. My heartfelt thanks go to the editor of *Anthropology and Humanism* and the anonymous reviewers of this manuscript. Without your assistance, this piece of writing would not be as clear and concise as it now appears. Of course, whatever faults remain are solely the fault of the author. I also thank the American Anthropological Association for permission to use this paper in a revised format for this volume.

2. A slightly different version of this chapter was published in *Anthropology and Humanism*, 44(2): 293–305. Special thanks to David Syring and the editors at *Anthropology and Humanism* as well as the editors at Lexington Books, including Kasey Beduhn for their help in developing this article.

3. It is worth noting that while Texas did permit concealed carry in 1995, the state did not enact an open-carry law for handguns until 2015. Whether this was my embellishment or theirs, I honestly cannot say.

4. Atlanta hosted the summer Olympics in 1996. As with every Olympic city in the modern era, Atlanta spent heavily on infrastructure projects and gentrification. Five Points, a region known for its night-life, was targeted in the process and made more "tourist friendly."

REFERENCES

Abelmann, Nancy. 1997. "Narrating Selfhood and Personality in South Korea: Women and Social Mobility." *American Ethnologist*, 24(4): 786–812.

Battaglia, Debbora. 1995. "Problematizing the Self: A Thematic Introduction." In *Rhetorics of Self-Making*, edited by Debbora Battaglia. Berkeley, CA: University of California Press.

Baudrillard, Jean. 1996. *The Perfect Crime*, Translated by Chris Turner. New York, NY: Verso.

Bhimull, Chandra D. 2014. "Passages: Airborne in an African Diaspora." *Anthropology and Humanism*, 39(2): 129–144.

Bourgois, Philippe. 2003. *In Search of Respect: Selling Crack in El Barrio.* Cambridge: Cambridge University Press.

Bruner, Edward. 1986. "Experience and Its Expressions." In *The Anthropology of Experience*, edited by Victor W. Turner and Edward Bruner, 3–30. Urbana, IL: University of Illinois Press.

_____. 1993. "Introduction: The Ethnographic Self and the Personal Self." In *Anthropology and Literature*, edited by Paul Benson, 1–25. Urbana, IL and Chicago, IL: University of Illinois Press.

Fabian, Johannes. 1983. *Time and the Other: How Anthropology Makes Its Other.* New York, NY: Columbia University Press.

Friedman, Jonathan. 1994. *Cultural Identity and Global Process.* London: Sage.

Jameson, Fredric. 1991. *Postmodernism, or, The Cultural Logic of Late Capitalism.* Durham, NC: Duke University Press.

Lyotard, Jean-Francois. 1984 "The Postmodern Condition: A Report on Knowledge." In *Theory and History of Literature*, Vol. 10, 1st edition. Translated by Geoff Bennington and Brian Massumi. Minneapolis, MN: University of Minnesota Press.

Mortensen Lena and George Nicholas. 2010. "Riding the Tourism Train? Navigating Intellectual Property, Heritage and Community-Based Approaches to Cultural Tourism." *Anthropology News*, November 2010: 11–12.

Radhakrishnan, R. 1996. *Diasporic Meditations: Between Home and Location.* Minneapolis, MN and London: University of Minnesota Press.

Rosaldo, Michelle Zimbalist. 1980. *Knowledge and Passion: Illongot Notions of Self and Social Life.* Cambridge, MA: Cambridge University Press.

Rorty, Amelie Oksenberg. 1976. "A Literary Postscript: Characters, Persons, Selves, Individuals." In *Identities of Persons*, edited by Amelie Oksenberk Rorty, 301–323. Berkeley, CA: University of California Press.

Said, Edward. 1993. *Culture and Imperialism.* London: Chatto and Windus.

Schweder, Richard A. 1991. *Thinking through Cultures: Expeditions in Cultural Psychology.* Cambridge, MA: Harvard University Press.

Seremetakis, C. Nadia. 1994. *The Senses Still: Perception and Memory as Material Culture in Modernity.* Chicago, IL: University of Chicago Press.

Steedly, Mary Margaret. 1993. *Hanging without a Rope: Narrative Experiences in Colonial and Postcolonial Karoland.* Princeton, NJ: Princeton University Press.

Somers, Margaret R. 1994. "The Narrative Constitution of Identity: A Relational and Network Approach." *Theory and Society* 23: 605–649.

Stewart, Kathleen. 1996. *A Space on the Side of the Road: Cultural Poetics in an "Other" America.* Princeton, NJ: Princeton University Press.

_____. 2017. "In the World that Affect Proposed." *Cultural Anthropology*, 32(2): 192–198.

Stoller, Paul. 2007. "Ethnography/Memoir/Imagination/Story." *Anthropology and Humanism*, 32(2): 178–191.

Syring, David and Julia Offen. 2017. "Sudden Anthropology: Brief Encounters with Cultures." *Anthropology and Humanism*, 42(1): 5–6.

Tanaka, Greg. 2009. "The Elephant in the Living Room that No One wants to Talk About: Why U.S. Anthropologists Are Unable to Acknowledge the End of Culture." *Anthropology and Education Quarterly*, 40(1): 82–95.

Tsing, Anna. 1993. *In the Realm of the Diamond Queen: Marginality in an Out-of-the-Way Place*. Princeton, NJ: Princeton University Press.

Turner, Edith. 2008. "Introduction to the Art of Ethnography." *Anthropology and Humanism*, 32(2): 108–116.

Vannini, Philip. 2011. "Mind the Gap: The *tempo rubato* of Dwelling in Lineups." *Mobilities*, 6(2): 273–299.

_____. 2015. "Non-Representational Research Methodologies: An Introduction." In *Non-Representational Methodologies: Re-Envisioning Research*, edited by Phillip Vannini, 1–18. New York, NY: Routledge.

Chapter 4

Alabama

Derek Pardue

I always struggled with the questions of "Who are you?" and "Where are you from?" I mean, of course, few people phrase it that way. "Uh, excuse me, but who are you (again)?" And, yet, it is the basis of all interactions, isn't it? I mean, we start out with assumptions and stereotypes. We size up each other. We check our own selves in the bathroom, at the door, in the car, on the subway, right before a big meeting, out on a date. And, all of that in a place we are more or less familiar with. Our hometown. On campus. In a big city, we visit friends and family. Spend the holidays. Go to a show. We put it all somehow into a context. I guess we get used to all of that over time. Sometimes, though, things happen when we go abroad and get outside of our little bubbles of common sense.

This essay is about taking chances, feeling strange, and trying to learn something about self and others. It's about confronting one's past, particularly those embarrassing elements that inevitably emerge when you least expect it. I learned that sometimes those uncomfortable truths can become a resource; they are never entirely resolved but do not remain exclusively negative or void of value. It's one of those things that anthropological fieldwork often conjures as it forces us to reflect seriously on identity (or better, identification) and all the rich mess surrounding that ongoing process.

This story *takes* place in what is now a city I call "home," even though I don't live there anymore. I visit every year; I have nostalgia. This story is *about* a place I have never lived but is officially part of me and is deeply rooted in my family's history. I was born *there* and it is possible that there is a grave plot with my name on it. This story is also a small slice of urban anthropology. It's about "going into the field." Let me explain.

São Paulo is a megacity, a chaotic area with roughly twenty million inhabitants. One out of every ten Brazilians lives in the São Paulo metro area and over 50 percent of these dwellers live in something called the *periferia*, and a variable portion of this area can be defined as some sort of slum. Many English speakers nowadays recognize the term *favela*. That gives you an idea of the weight of what we're talking about. For the most part, my experience in São Paulo over the past twenty-five years has taken place in these areas accompanied by local hip-hoppers (rappers, DJs, graffiti artists, street dancers) as well as newly arrived West African and Haitian immigrants and their growing networks.

A story is never *just* a story. There are signs, keywords, gestures, contexts and intentions. We, as readers, generate multiple meanings even in the most banal or straightforward of tales, as this one is. What might we take away from fieldwork experience as potential knowledge? How might we give structure to what we learn from an experience of difference?

The reality is that it is impossible to prepare entirely for going into the field as a (burgeoning) anthropologist. Many university departments rightly concern themselves over providing competencies in language, methodology and theory. Administrators in places like the United States apply for federal or state grants to hire language teachers in underserved languages such as Aymara, Arabic, Hindi, Portuguese, Swahili, Urdu, and Wolof. We become excited and increasingly inquisitive about this something, this somewhere outside of our norm.

"Alabama" begins with a reflection on identity—"Who are you"? We learn, for example, some details of the complex identity of Nikki as a Japanese-American woman. Of course, this sort of hybridity is increasingly more common throughout the world and each society has developed a variety of ways, including formalized legislation and ideologically based discrimination, to make sense of such realities. But, yeah, sorry, no spoilers, let me share this little *gringo* story. Ultimately, I suggest that identity stories and reflections on "the field" are invariably related to each other and offer humble beginnings to a much larger conversation. Please take this as an invitation to expand, historicize, contextualize, debate, and apply elsewhere.

* * *

Nikki and I were not really friends. We had mutual friends. Like at parties we would be in the same conversations chatting about music and why high school (and later, college) was such a joke. Theo enjoyed dropping random names of avenues in New York City. Darlene had an acute sense of California beaches. I tried my best to remember some landmark of the various places I had moved. And, yet, here we all were back in Huntsville, Alabama. For better or worse, the birthplace of everyone still standing.

Nikki always hung around a wild white girl named Sally, whose laughter can be best described as "whooping and hollering." I could never figure out if she was drunk all the time or if it was all just her nature. Our mutual friend was Dave, my entrée into the local punk rock scene. "What a waste of time" was the usual takeaway from these scenes. Of course, nobody was really there for the content of discussion, right?

Nikki was drop dead gorgeous, at least to me. She intimidated the hell out of me. I could barely look her in the eye. I think it was around this time that I started to use the word "striking" on a regular basis in my vocabulary. Nikki's father was Japanese, an immigrant kid caught up in the violent nonsense of California detention camps during the war. He grew up in that mess, survived, studied and became an engineer, moved around to different military bases to work for the government that had imprisoned him and his immediate family. Only in the United States. Well, not really, but some of that contradiction was not lost on Nikki. After years of growing up here and there, being called "white," "Asian," not quite this and not quite that, she developed a manner of taking over conversations. Sally's boisterous yelps and guffawing made it all a spectacle. Taken together, honestly, I didn't mind sitting back and watching it all unfold.

Nikki stirred the pot, "Hey Dave, did you see this article about this Dominican guy in New York?" Dave and I were deep in debate about how derivative certain bands were. That night it was about The Cramps versus Bad Brains. I laid into him, "I mean, The Cramps are all garage rockabilly with an edge. Then, you have a hardcore outfit like BB that does roots reggae too. That's genius. End of story." I could see Dave's eyes bulge preparing to speak his mind about how "all bands are derivative and there is no genius." Dave isn't most people and his way with words always provided memorable moments. He was a master of the turn of the phrase, but he never got the chance that night, though.

Nikki insisted, "Davie, listen. This guy gets off the plane in JFK. Picks up his bags and whatever and proceeds to customs. He is stopped and asked where he was staying. The man said, 'Manhattan, around Central Park, the Ritz-Carlton.' Then, the agent 'right, are you a celebrity or something? Not many Black folks can afford to stay there.' The man looked at the agent sternly and blurted out, 'I am not Black. I am Dominican.' The agent, 'n—a, you darker than me. Just get outta here and, uh, welcome to the United States.' See, that's what I'm talking about."

Everyone looked around at each other, me included, seemingly with the same expression of "What exactly are you talking about, Nikki?" No one dared to verbalize. She continued, "the DR, Colombia, Brazil. I have always wanted to go visit . . . Sally and I are going. Who's with us?"

Memory is funny sometimes. It can be simultaneously surprisingly detailed and nuanced as well as vague and misleading. There are always gaps. Blackouts. People say drugs and alcohol dissolve memory. I don't buy that. Maybe they have an effect. I like to think of such substances as shaping devices rather than superficial erasers. In any case, I am not exactly sure how I substituted Sally, but after a couple of nervous, awkward phone calls, Nikki and I met at a Circle K convenience store on the corner of Jordan and Holmes in Hunstville, Alabama. Davie had dropped me off and bought me a Sprite for the road. Nikki and I smoked and drank continuously as we jumped from one classic rock radio station to the next. It's surprising how many of those songs you just know.

Nikki and I drove through the night. Destination: Miami. We had open-ended tickets made out of layered, pastel-colored paper. The little booklet looked funny and despite its small size, it turned out to quite cumbersome. I recall carbon paper floating around always on the brink of falling out of place and somehow invalidating the whole trip.

São Paulo. Brazil. Still groggy, the city struggled to shirk the early morning fog. The smell of tropical dew greeted us as we exited the plane and ventured into that no-man's land of asphalt and curious motorized vehicles in between the airplane and the terminal. The sun was just getting started and I was relieved to feel a slight breeze. Even inside the airport there were natural corridors of air. After shivering to death inside the plane all night, I had sworn off air conditioning and this all just felt right. Nikki, disheveled with the pattern of the airplane seat upholstery still imprinted on her right cheek and yet still remarkably stunning, sat down next to me in plastic bucket seats bolted to a black steel frame. We waited for our luggage. She smiled weakly at me and I returned the favor, feeling as if we were equal partners in a crime, the details of which neither one could remember. I looked down to see that ketchup was splattered across my bright yellow "Banned in DC" T-shirt in homage to the live album of Bad Brains. The flow of ketchup had splintered from the original stain and over the course of the trip had taken on social and political meanings as it was juxtaposed to the rendering of the White House. Red on yellow on Black and white. Murder in the capital city. Lightning strikes. Down with the system. A revolutionary in my own mind. "That's fucking cool," I thought to myself and wondered if Nikki's smile was in recognition of my punk aesthetic. I sat up and wiped my tongue across my upper teeth in preparation to snag our bags. And, there I felt it, strands of spinach lingering behind. Most certainly Nikki was laughing *at* me. I shook it off, as Nikki ran a brush through her hair.

And, then, as our bags appeared, hers leaning on mine as if for support, it really hit us; we had no idea what was in store. Our research for the trip consisted of flipping through a dog-eared copy of a Fodor's guide to Brazil. I think. I don't know. One of those things that one might find in a San Francisco coffee shop in the early 1990s. In a hostel. A book for daydreaming and a book of reference. A book with currency conversion rates. A book that has to be updated for reasons I discovered upon arrival as a foreigner in this massive city in a country whose language of Portuguese looked kind of familiar, you know like Spanish, but remained incomprehensible.

The harsh realities of a new currency, the Brazilian "*Real*," were not mentioned in the guide book. The brief consult had put me at ease when I noticed that one U.S. dollar was worth several million *cruzados*. No worries, right? But, the "*real*" was pinned to the U.S. dollar and when we arrived it was actually stronger than the dollar. I was immediately poor and lost and all this confusion quickly drove a wedge in between Nikki and me. She left for Rio and points north and I bunkered up in a *pensão*, or in Spanish Latin America a *pensión*. A bunk bed in a room full of day laborers, recovering alcoholics and men simply getting from one day to the next. I learned Portuguese in a hurry. Within two months I spoke a heavily, gringo-accented street Portuguese. But this story is not about that. In the end, it's about Alabama. You'll see. I remember looking at that pastel paper sandwich airline ticket with its tattered carbon meat hanging out one last time before I chucked it into the trash. I was determined not to return to the United States.

I *did* have a plan. Seriously. A vague, humble plan of getting to know the hip-hop scene in São Paulo, a place I discovered was the center of rap and hip-hop in Brazil. My plan, in retrospect, was *fieldwork*. Before social media, there were things called flyers. They were material posters attached (by any means necessary) to billboards however big or small. Record stores were and, in a significant way, have returned to be central depositories of flyers. And, therein my discovery of the MNU, the United Black Movement or *Movimento Negro Unificado*, unfolded.

I wasn't really looking for them per se. I saw a small, simple flyer stating that a series of rap groups representing the Posse Hausa would be performing at this place in São Bernardo do Campo, an industrial city in the metro area of São Paulo. The MNU sponsored the event. Perfect. I had been to college and read enough to catch the reference to the West African ethnic group in the word, Hausa or Haussa. And, then, there was the São Bernardo reference, which I would understand later to be a strong reference to the metal worker unions and accompanying sociopolitical movements, from which the famous labor leader, future populist president and the ultimate target of current Brazilian fascism, Lula emerged. Not to mention the obvious Black nationalism embedded in the MNU acronym. Race, class, regional and national politics, cultural nationalism, the show had everything going for it.

By this time, I had begun to comprehend Portuguese to a level where I could read the newspaper and get the gist of simple stories. Folklore. Popular histories. Seemingly, every day something would happen that I did not understand and it provoked me to try and fill in the gap. I still have plenty of gaps but I had begun to make progress in building a base of knowledge, a kind of cultural competency. Most of the time, I got tired of feeling like an idiot.

The show was to take place on a Saturday afternoon and as the date approached, I became increasingly nervous. What the hell am I trying to accomplish anyway? "It's just a show. I'll hang out for an hour or so, check the sounds and I'm gone. It's no different than any other show, right?" I thought to myself. I mouthed the words. I said them in Portuguese. I practiced the most mundane responses to questions of intent. *O que você tá fazendo aqui? O que você quer?* (What are you doing here? What do you want?). I wrote keywords and phrases down on paper. I believed that this would help me remember stuff. The connection between thought, words, memory, familiarity, confidence, and flow. Writing it down would facilitate all of that. I still think it is true. You know, lecture slides, conference papers, notes for any presentation.

The locale was the former labor union building of the São Bernardo metal-workers. A nondescript, three-story building on the corner of two residential streets near the bus/tram terminal of Ferrazópolis, a gateway station that opens up to the massive automobile plants of Volkswagen and Brasmotor. A reminder of a modernizing Brazil. A postwar initiative. A promise of employment and infrastructure. I never visited these plants. One can only really appreciate the size of such lots from aerial photographs and from certain locations in Jardim Silvina and other more recent improvised housing communities that coat the surrounding hills like scales on a reptile.

A young rapper and occasional fieldwork consultant once described the urban periphery in São Paulo as "leftovers" *(restos)*. The rest. Nothing is really new; it is all recycled. Looks that way, too. People repurpose electrical wire, copper, planks of wood, rainwater, and fabric. They invite family and friends over for a barbeque with the goal of, at some point, pouring cement, and thus inaugurating their new home. A palette of grays and browns provide a backdrop to the visual screams out in the wind. Residents erect bold, forest green banners or massive black and white murals featuring logos and mascots to support their football teams, Palmeiras, Corinthians, Santos, and São Paulo. Local entrepreneurs hire or cajole local teen graffiti artists or that kid everyone knows who sits at home or on the corner all day sketching imaginary comic book characters. "Draw some Disney figures eating pizza," they say. "Why is Goofy a unicorn?" they later complain.

The periphery is full of imaginative commercial hybrids. My favorite is a clever twist on McDonalds called "Mané Donald's." While the name deserves its own academic analysis, suffice it to say that the name incorporates one of the most common nicknames in Brazil and one of the most common mistakes among Brazilians in relation to English. The fetishization of the apostrophe reveals a desire for class mobility and, yet, the establishment serves mediocre baked goods. Knockoff brands composed of not quite authentic color schemes fill the periphery landscape. In São Bernardo such popular scenarios run up against the immediately recognizable corporate typography and design of German automobiles. Precious.

I studied the maps, plotted my trip, counted out exact change and promptly fell asleep on the "trolley bus" that traversed the municipal borders and demanded its own ticket. I woke up disoriented and remarkably identified the Habib's corporate sign (faux Middle Eastern fast-food franchise with a seriously racist mascot). I had reached my destination, or so I thought. Habib's popularity rivals that of McDonalds (as well as Mané Donald's) and thus there are hundreds of Habib stores and, well, I got off the bus at the wrong Habib about a mile too early.

Dusk began to transform the early spring sky into a hazy orange. Where the subtropical sun had only minutes before been able to overcome the pollutants in the air and make its presence known in a blare, there was now an increasing opacity. A growing pixilation of reality. I found it difficult to focus and stumbled on the curb exhausted from my two-hour journey southeast of downtown São Paulo, far from my shitty but comfortable *pensão*, where men slept on bunk beds and talked *futebol* (soccer) in the dark and whistled out the window at imaginary girls and passed putrid gas in the middle of the night.

I heard nothing as I finally arrived at the union building. I checked the address three, four, five times. I walked around the block thinking there might be a secret, awesome entrance. A tunnel filled with avant-garde graffiti leading to the mad funk palace of rhymes and beats. Fresh kids spinning on heads and mixing capoeira with old school electric boogaloo. The stomping and screaming of style was simply barricaded, temporarily locked away underground. I just needed to find the special entrance. It's gotta be around here somewhere.

Of course, that's a fucking dream. Shit is rarely if ever like that. Then perhaps this story would be entitled "tunnel of fun" or something horrific like that. Something Disney-esque like that. No, it's called "Alabama" for a reason.

I had cased the joint and there was no alternative entrance. This was it. There was a lone light bulb off in the distance inside down the hall. The door was open. I walked in. "Geez, I'm here now," I thought to myself. Maybe there's a pile of cool labor posters on a folding card table where Lula used to play domino or some wicked alloy metal contraption, one of José's legendary "projects" turning the poor guy into the butt of all too many jokes. Maybe something like that was lying around that I could use as an ashtray or a paperweight. Some keepsake. A souvenir for my troubles. I walked down the corridor toward the light.

One voice, then another voice, slightly more nasal. Another, more guttural. Several voices now vying for the right to speak. The one word uttered over and over again was *irmão* or brother. I hesitated before entering and yet felt compelled to go ahead and walk into a room of total strangers with no apparent show, no apparent reason for being there and no real idea what I was going to say. As soon as I opened the door, I forgot everything and smiled. "Act like you know," a phrase from Rakim or Nas or KRS-1 or some golden era rapper that stuck with me. I walked in and sat down on a plastic bar stool and turned my attention to the speaker.

All eyes *were* on me. My head flooded with U.S. hip-hop references. Far from the heights of Tupac's fame and amazing charisma, I sat there. A white, blue-eyed man, a former grad student from the University of Texas at Austin, in a labor headquarters cafeteria. The egg yolk yellow of the dangling light bulb became a flaming spotlight. A serpent of the revolution raised up and dedicated all of its energy into a scorching ray meant to sear the truth out of me.

"Excuse me, are you lost? Can I help you?" The middle-aged man, whose discourse I had interrupted with my completely unexpected entrance, had finished his point about the importance of recruitment of young Black warriors in the periphery neighborhoods. This was, in fact, the underlying motivation of today's show. "Rap, hip-hop, you know. It's what the youth are into," he said. And, he continued, "We are excited to hear the messages of our young brothers and sisters from Posse Hausa." He gestured stage left and I saw a group of a dozen Black teenagers. A few with calm, knowing smiles on their faces and others nervously looking at their Chuck Taylor Converse high tops.

"Yeah, sorry. I came for the show. I came to see Posse Hausa." I sat up ridiculously straight on the stool in an effort to keep my confidence but simultaneously reinforcing all sorts of stereotypes of white stiffness. No flow.

"Right. But, this is also a meeting of the MNU, too. Did you know that?" The guy now was leaning into me. Questioning my presence. At that moment, a member of the audience stood up. I recognized him. We had drunk beer recently somewhere near Paulista Avenue, the Wall Street of São Paulo. He was finishing his masters degree in sociology or anthropology at the University of São Paulo. One, if not the only, Black Brazilian on campus. Most Black folks are Nigerian, Angolan or Cape Verdean exchange students. Africans of means. Gabriel had explained his thesis to me and I pretended that I understood him and his supposed radical theories of critical race theory and gender. I certainly didn't have the linguistic chops for that at the time. I weathered the storm, drank and unintentionally (or intentionally, who knows?) forgot all about it the next day. Except for his look. A big guy. Massive dreads. Boisterous. Older than me, I guess. I am not very good at those things, but, yeah, definitely not a kid anymore.

"Brother, this is Derek. He's American. He came here to conduct research. Derek, why don't you tell us about your project? And, then, we'll set up for Posse Hausa."

Nightmare. On my best days, back then I could handle simple statements, like "this food is delicious" or "I wonder who will win the next World Cup." I had already said that I had come to see the show. Discuss my research? Where would I find the vocabulary? Where was my pitch? My accent was horrible. No one will understand me. Thanks a lot *brother*. House of cards.

There was a moment of silence, I read as an approval or an anticipation of some sort, followed by a staggered series of scrapes and slides as the audience turned their chairs and positioned themselves to hear, in essence, my project description.

This was a disaster. You know what, I am never going to see these people again, I thought to myself. I am never going to be able to articulate myself in complete phrases. I stood up, closed my eyes and lifted my head to make no mistake.

"I AM FROM ALABAMA. MY FAMILY IS ALL FROM ALABAMA AND GEORGIA."

A chorus of "oohs" and "umphs" erupted from the small crowd. As I imagined, these folks had read about the civil rights movement in the United States and the word "Alabama," especially, was like "Auschwitz." They were aghast. The enemy was brazenly present. The nerve, right? Wtf?

I could have said, "Well, you know, as I learned from Karuna Maliki, a senior officer in the Oakland Black Panther Party, the path revolution travels links the city and the country, the north and south. The continents will come back together as they once were in the time of *Mulungu*, the Swahili, African-Arabic term for God, the creator. The path is 'shining' and I am but a humble messenger searching with all of you for a better way." I could have said that (with some help perhaps from Gabriel, the masters student who was content to sit off to the side. An island of laughter. His own entertainment center). Maybe, I should have. It would have been partly true, partly elaborated from a shared experience, partly a wish, a curse, a premonition. Like everything we say.

But, I didn't say any of that. In fact, the little sentence I stumbled through regarding my birthplace and my family roots was all I managed to communicate to the group as a whole. Most of them had made up their mind and noisily turned their seats back around facing the stage. Fair enough. There is no denying the histories and legacies of white supremacy and state-sponsored violence against Black and brown people. "Alabama" is a touchstone for an American nightmare that connects to similar racism in Brazil, the largest importer of African slaves (by far!!), the Caribbean, much of Latin America, Portugal, other points in Europe, and more recently Dubai and cities in India and China. Why on earth would I lead off with that little tidbit about myself? Talk about not reading my audience, right?

I am not gonna lie. I was shattered and immediately regretted what I said and the whole affair. But, as it happened, after I sat back down and the proceedings continued, the shade gradually lifted. A couple of the members of Posse Hausa approached me and asked blankly if that was really true. It was a question of opening; "Who are you, *really*?" was the subtext. In the small group, patience was more easily achieved. We exchanged stories. And, while the awkwardness never really disappeared, they did ask for my phone number (landline, no cells or Internet back then, I know, I'm old) and handed me a flyer for an upcoming show featuring dozens of rap groups, including the two main artists from the Posse Hausa—Banzu Bantu (another reference to a major African ethnic group) and The Alchemists (*Os Alquimistas*). I stay in touch with most of them until today.

* * *

The concept of identity has had a conflicted history in anthropology, specifically, and in the social sciences and the humanities, more generally. In great part, the tension stems from the idea of "identity" as a static category, which is the commonplace notion of the term highlighted in formal documents such as national census reports (e.g., "Alabama" as my birthplace, printed on virtually all of my official document), and the idea of "identity" as a set of dynamic practices that people do to make claims in the world and feel a part of a group. I was always felt closer to The Alchemists in this regard. They experimented, blending jazz with rap, odd house beats with abstract lyrics. They were rough and weird and loved De La Soul. Or, in today's scene, they might be compared to R.A.P. Ferreira or even JPEGMAFIA.

One of the identification processes in play within the story above is an articulation of Blackness. Organizations such as the MNU and reference points such as Alabama contribute to an identification that involves multiple places. The current moment of intense migration is with regard to not only people but also ideas and symbols. In the end, this provided me with an entrée into the field, albeit emotionally trying. I would take this perspective of Blackness and later develop it, informed by fieldwork in Lisbon, Portugal and Praia, Cape Verde, and then back in São Paulo, to argue that Blackness is constituted through mobility.

The story is a wax and wane, a series of back and forth, conquests and failures. Identification takes place. Alchemy requires a certain mobility of things. Parteum, a former professional skateboarder and current hip-hop producer, met many of the members of the Posse Hausa around the time I did, in the mid-1990s at the massive half-pipe located near the central bus terminal. I have inserted excerpts from a fieldwork conversation we had in 2009. They are worth quoting here, because they speak directly to the productive relationship between city space, objects and humanity, implicit in "Alabama."

"You are part of the city even when you ignore it . . . We don't realize how connected we are to the space we occupy . . . I just try to bring elements that call attention to this puzzle in my music . . . It doesn't always make sense at first, but it is a true register and, you know, it has to be complex in order to represent what the city is. A city, any street, any hotel room, any library, any subway car, any bus stop inspires, and I have to believe that there exists a reciprocity between a person and that object."

Similar to Parteum's artistic trajectory, I as an urban anthropologist find myself between strong traditions of representation. Is the city best characterized as a set of institutions and patterns of demographic shifts, or is it best captured as experience? Similarly, is identification best understood as a set of categories or a series of achievements? Are these even fair questions? Perhaps, it is all a mixture of both and we must consider identity and place on a case-by-case basis. Over the years, scholars have held differing opinions on these issues. For my part, I take a cue from Parteum and hope to provide a feeling for São Paulo and self/other through reflection on the material and imaginary as always in critical dialogue. And, with this said, the idea of "Alabama" has changed, expanded and been repurposed. Like everything we say. The story doesn't really end here.

Chapter 5

Friends, Family, Informants

Fieldwork as Relationship

Angela Glaros

A FRIEND TO OPEN THE DOOR

"You're feeling frustrated, aren't you, because you can't get anyone to talk to you?" "N" (a pseudonym to preserve her confidentiality) asked me over coffee. It was January 30, 2008, the feast of the Three Holy Hierarchs (Basil the Great, Gregory the Theologian, and John Chrysostom), and the liturgy had just ended in the church of the Panayia Melikarou on the Greek island of Skyros. January 30 is a school holiday in Greece, as the Three Hierarchs are patron saints of higher education, so my son Dimitri's preschool was closed. Few of his classmates had been in church, though his teacher was there and remarked on his good church behavior. On our way out, she introduced me to N, who invited me for coffee while Dimitri ran around the square just across the narrow street. I told N about my dissertation research on the island's songs. Remarkably, she immediately keyed in on my difficulties; perhaps she could read them on my face.

We had been living on Skyros full time since the autumn of 2007 at that point, and as yet I had not been able to hear live singing, nor had I been able to meet with or interview any singers. In fact, I was beginning to notice a practiced sense of secrecy surrounding traditional vocal music on Skyros. While the island's expressive culture—in particular, its tradition of Carnival masquerade and satire—is well-known in and beyond Greece, my project focused on a lesser-known but locally prized musical form, the unaccompanied table songs (*traghoudhia tis tavlas*) performed on festive occasions. Table songs are marked by highly ornamented melodies that share musical modes with Byzantine liturgical chant and demand skilled and virtuosic performance. While the islanders prized their songs, they also spoke of them as endangered or in a state of decline. I had assumed that this sense of endangerment would lend urgency to my research, and that Skyrians would open their doors to someone who wanted to shed light on their treasured traditions. Instead, I found those doors largely closed. Similar to what Page (1988) reported during her fieldwork in Granada, while Skyrians would readily talk to me *about* the songs, getting singers, particularly women singers, to agree to be interviewed or to have their voices recorded, proved more challenging.

I also struggled to establish any kind of musical apprenticeship on Skyros. Apprenticeship and performance have long been staples of ethnomusicological fieldwork (see, for example, Buchanan 2006; Hood 1960; Montell 1996; Rice 1994, 1997; Sugarman 1997). Nevertheless, finding a skilled singer to instruct me in the local musical style proved impossible. Before I even arrived on the island, local folklorist Aliki Lambrou (2004) explained over the telephone that Skyrians, and particularly the elders who knew the most songs, did not consider singing to be the kind of thing that could be formally taught. Indeed, several others told me, "Our songs can't be taught; they must be lived." It seemed that I could neither receive instruction in singing, nor hear the experts themselves perform the songs.

Given such difficulties, I shed a few tears of relief when N keyed in on my frustrations, and even more when she took me in hand, offering to introduce me to singers she knew, and even to "dress" me for Carnival—meaning that she would outfit me with traditional clothing for the Clean Monday dancing and feasting that marks the transition from Carnival to Lent. Indeed, in the months that followed, N introduced me to the local saint's day feasts (*paneyiria*) held in tiny country chapels, where I finally heard Skyrian songs performed live and began to understand their social meaning. While not all of her plans came to fruition, N's friendship did, in fact, open many doors that had previously been closed, and through my association with her, other Skyrians began to make sense of me—albeit in some unexpected ways.

I tell my students about meeting N when I discuss ethnographic fieldwork, noting that the friendships and close working relationships that anthropologists form with "key informants" in the field lead to small insights and enormous breakthroughs, and above all, create shared narratives that help them become legible to the communities in which they conduct research (Kisliuk 1997). Indeed, as I explain, ethnographic fieldwork centers on developing relationships of trust. When our interlocutors in the field witness our own relationships, whether with family members who accompany us to the field, or with community members who befriend us, it helps them to forge their own relationships with us. Relationships are key to understanding the human condition; if this were not so, kinship would not form such a crucial part of most traditional ethnographic accounts.

What I neglect to point out in these lectures is that I had not expected to *need* someone like N to provide entry into the community. I had naively thought that my Greek-American status as a "halfie" (Abu-Lughod 1991) would serve to make me familiar to locals, even as arriving on the island with a cute preschooler would endear both of us to them and provide an immediate opening gambit to conversations. Instead, while my ethnicity and fluency in Greek garnered me enough respect that people spoke to me in Greek rather than English, I largely felt isolated and marginalized, in part because my son had such a difficult time adjusting. He threw tantrums in stores, rejected the candy offered by friendly Skyrians, and acted up at preschool—as anyone might have predicted, since he joined in the middle of the year and spoke no Greek. "Mama, I don't have language power here," he complained to me.

I had signed my son up for preschool thinking that while he was there in the mornings, I could arrange interviews with singers. As I soon learned, however, no one wanted to meet in the mornings, since that was the time for Skyrians (especially women) to take care of housework, cooking, and errands. Early evening, after the midday siesta, was the time for visits, including research-related visits. As luck would have it, my son also chose this period to stop taking afternoon naps, so that now he slept from 6:00 p.m. to 6:00 a.m. every day, and I was effectively on house arrest precisely during visiting time, because I had also not been able to locate any child care providers. To say that I didn't plan for this aspect of my fieldwork as a single mother is putting it mildly. As a result, I had spent the first few months of the winter holed up in my house, listening to field recordings of Skyrian songs from published books; as it turned out, however, this was excellent preparation for what was to come, though at the time it felt like an utter failure.

Given my situation, when N came on the scene I eagerly accepted her offer of help. So it was that by early February 2008, I found myself squeezed into an old car with a group of women, bouncing along bumpy country roads to my first festival on the feast day of St. Haralambos. We arrived after the liturgy, since I had needed to drop Dimitri at preschool and N needed to locate a ride, but we did arrive in time to light a candle in the chapel and join the feasting in the small refectory (*art'kas*) next door, and to wait for the singing to begin. After a few hours, we departed so I could pick Dimitri up and get home. I had managed to engage in a research activity while my son was at preschool, which felt like a major triumph.

THROUGH THE EYES OF OTHERS

While N was not my first research contact (I had already spoken to Aliki Lambrou, though we did not meet in person until mid-March of that year), she was the first person to actively put me in contact with the musical life of Skyros. The festivals I attended with her opened my eyes to the intimate, and yet still technically public, encounters with local songs they offered. N was an excellent guide and ambassador at these events, reminding me to wear running shoes to climb steep hillsides at some festivals, and always introducing me to people. At a church service, she once described me to the priest as a "music professor," which was generous, if untrue.

My friendship with N, however, was met with surprise and consternation on the part of other Skyrians. The most common reaction to our friendship was "Why are you talking to her? She doesn't know any songs." People warned me to watch out for her: "She's crazy, you know." It appeared that, while she fulfilled the role of "key informant" in my field research, N occupied a somewhat marginal position in her own society. People told me stories about her past behavior, the spiritual visions she claimed to experience (often involving St. George, the patron saint of Skyros), her attachment to religion and her eager participation in religious feasts and processions. While her fellow islanders found this behavior abnormal, that very focus on religion gave N a thorough knowledge of the festivals, which was ultimately of great value to me—and not only to me. In June, for example, we visited Manos Faltaits (2006), a prominent local folklorist, archaeologist, and museum director. That evening, he and his wife asked N to recite the names, locations, and festival dates of all the small country chapels (*ksoklisia*) that she could recall. It was apparent that her knowledge was prodigious. And in fact, when I reminded concerned Skyrians that N knew about all the festivals, and that going to the festivals allowed me to hear songs, they had to admit that this was true. There was no denying, however, that my association with N changed their views of me, and caused them to question whether I was conducting my study in the "right" way, since I was willing to speak to community members who were not recognized as official authorities on Skyrian music. These reactions were themselves instructive, since they helped me to see how Skyrians framed their local songs as a carefully guarded form of knowledge. Becoming legible to the community through my association with N was risky, but ultimately rewarding.

NEGOTIATING THE BOND

As anyone might have predicted, my friendship with N also held more personal challenges. Her very desire to take me in hand meant that at times I felt like I was not in charge of my own project, and I came to agree with others regarding the intensity of her personal convictions, even though they never seemed "crazy" to me. I also began to experience the kinds of cultural clashes that we expect in the field, but that had eluded me before, when all my relationships with locals had remained at arm's length. For example, N felt free to offer her opinions and criticisms of my weight, regardless of the fact that she herself had lost a great deal of weight in the recent past and would still not have been considered thin. Sometimes she would even greet me by saying "Hey fatty!" (*Ela, hontri!*) which, while uttered in friendliness, nonetheless irritated and embarrassed me; Gustafsson (2009) reports a similar experience while conducting fieldwork in Vietnam. However, I had years of experience dealing with the Greek combination of frankness and fatphobia that makes it challenging, not to mention infuriating, to be a fat person trying to travel or live in Greece; I also recognized that if I were very thin, people would simply comment on that instead. N's remarks ultimately reminded me that women's bodies were always under scrutiny in Greece (as elsewhere), and when I observed other Skyrians commenting on N's weight and reminding her not to gain back what she had lost, I saw that she and I were, in fact, both subject to the same gendered bodily scrutiny.

N also had a habit of asking me to give her my things. I had purchased a lot of items for the small house I rented: bedding, towels, rugs, a small television, a space heater. She asked me outright for all of the bedding once I left, because after all, I wouldn't be taking it with me back to the United States. And once, at the meal following the religious festival at her own family's chapel, she literally asked me for the shirt off my back, a top I had purchased while in Greece. As a Greek-American raised with understated Midwestern values, but who was also familiar with the frankness of many Greeks, I tried to negotiate such requests tactfully. In the end, I did leave N most of my bedding, but the top returned home with me. Twelve years later, her requests look to me like an index of the presumed closeness of our relationship, but also of the real economic plight of many Greeks at that time, and particularly rural islanders, who might own or inherit land, but who were also cash-poor and often unemployed. For example, I learned that not everyone owned a copy of the books that had recently been published on Skyrian music (Chianis 2003; Lambrou 2004); at 40 or 50 euros each (close to $60–75 at the time), not everyone could afford such extravagance, even if the books helped to preserve their endangered song traditions. Again, my relationship with N made the everyday circumstances of many islanders concretely real for me, even as it echoed the experience of many field researchers who confront not only the sometimes-dire circumstances of the local community but also the radically different notions of property (Kisliuk 1997).

DAUGHTER AND NEIGHBOR

While my friendship with N represented a turning point in my research on Skyros, family was also essential to my progress. When my parents arrived in mid-February 2008 to spend the weeks of Carnival with us, I was finally able to leave the house in the evenings, participate in Carnival events, and attend other festivals that took place while preschool was on vacation. During their stay, I began to meet with Aliki, our first interview taking *six hours*. Additionally, my parents provided many Skyrians with yet another framework in which to understand me. I was not just a single mother with a rambunctious little boy; I was also a daughter. Once my parents departed again for the United States, people could inquire after them, and particularly after my stepfather, who spoke no Greek and yet somehow had conversations with locals without resorting to English. Their arrival also helped me to better understand some of the reticence of the locals to meet with me. I began to see that my gender might be an impediment at times. For example, my elderly male neighbor, the late Giannis Venardis, with whom I was on a cordial conversational basis, had never once invited me into his home. Yet he almost immediately invited my stepfather to visit. I considered that as a single, unmarried woman, my visits could be seen as scandalous.

My parents' visit, while helpful, also dramatically changed the course of my time in the field. After three weeks of being cared for by his grandparents, my son simply refused to return to preschool. As soon as our visas came through, I made the decision to take him back to the United States and return to Skyros on my own. By then it was April, and since my visa had a firm June 15 end date, the last two months of my fieldwork were the busiest. These months were a relief for the whole family: after such an intense period of straining to conduct fieldwork while meeting my son's needs, I was now free to focus on work at any time of the day or night. My parents, who had been helping me with childcare for five years, could again enjoy daily contact with their grandson, and my son, for his part, was so delighted to be back in the United States that when he saw my mother outside the baggage claim at the airport, he dropped everything and ran to her. These factors mitigated any loneliness I experienced while being separated from him.

After I returned to the island on my own, N continued to guide me to local festivals, and also brokered a change in my relationship with my neighbor, Mr. Venardis. I remember the day we came back from a festival we had attended a week after Easter and chatted with him in the street in front of our houses. N knew him well, and I noticed that she addressed him using the second person singular, instead of the more formal second person plural I had been using, and that he in turn had been using with me; such forms are the equivalent of the *tu/vous* distinction in French. I then handed him some blessed bread (*antidhoron*) from that morning's liturgy, and he told me, "I give *you* bread; you don't give *me* bread." It was true that he had developed a habit of stopping by my house to bring me bread after a liturgy if I had not made it to church. On this day, however, I stuck the bread in his pocket and ran inside my house so he couldn't refuse it. From that day on, we were on second person singular terms, a shift that N brokered for me and that led to a close working relationship with my neighbor. Not long after, Venardis invited me into his house, granted me interviews, and allowed me to record him singing traditional songs, including one that I have not found recorded in any previously published works on Skyrian music.

RESEARCH ASSISTANT

As I was planning my return to the United States, N offered to continue gathering data for me at local festivals and Carnival. She said she would attend these events and make recordings for me, so that I could get a sense of events I couldn't be present for. We made plans for what equipment she would need to carry this out, and we were both excited by the prospect. After I returned home, we had several Skype telephone conversations, and then few months later, I mailed her a digital camera that could record relatively short video segments, along with SD cards and an instruction manual. I never heard from her again. This may have been due to many factors, such as the economic crisis that engulfed Greece almost immediately after I returned to the United States in 2008, events in N's personal life that may have sent her to Athens instead of staying on the island, the "out of sight, out of mind" factor, or for all I know, my package may never have arrived. Due to my own move back to Illinois, dissertation writing, and my son's entry into kindergarten, I also failed to maintain contact with her beyond a few more letters and cards, none of which were answered.

It would be an exaggeration to say that my friendship with N alone was responsible for whatever progress I made in the field. After all, Aliki Lambrou was instrumental in my project, as were several other singers I met on my own (including one who approached me while I was out hanging laundry). But the day of our meeting did indeed mark a turning point for my fieldwork. N was the first Skyrian to bring me to a festival, and she was also the first to visit me in my home, the first to eat a meal I had prepared, the first to have personal conversations with me. Such acts of friendship and hospitality made me feel "real" in a fieldwork situation where I had felt mostly isolated, and for better or worse, helped me to become legible to the community as a whole. For these reasons, I introduce my students to N and describe our friendship, however transitory, whenever I talk about how fieldwork happens.

MOTHER AND APPRENTICE

After receipt of my PhD and the start of full-time academic work, I began a new project in 2013 on gender and Greek Orthodox liturgical music in east central Illinois. Given my background in the church and my involvement in church choirs since age fourteen, this research is about as "native" as an anthropological research project could be (Abu-Lughod 1991; Bargesian 2000; Narayan 1993). I have only recently begun to tell my students "field-work stories" from this project, in part because I have struggled to make sense of my position in the field, now that said field is the church I attend weekly. Many of my key informants, including area priests and chanters, were already friends or at least acquaintances, and sometimes fellow parishioners. However, the most surprising key informant has been my own son, now a high school senior, as well as an accomplished musician, composer, and liturgical chanter.

The process began several years ago when it became apparent that our church needed liturgical chanters. While a small choir sang responses along with the congregation during the liturgy, we lacked chanters to perform the matins (Orthros) service that precedes it, a service almost completely made up of sung or intoned verses that change weekly. The main chanter was in his nineties and not always able to attend, and others were college students or visiting scholars from Greece who came and went based on their schedules, or volunteers with very young children. This is a common situation at small parishes whose budgets do not allow them to hire chanters. Eventually my son volunteered to assist at these services and, following in the footsteps of generations of informally trained chanters in small communities, began an apprenticeship at the chanter's stand.

Meanwhile, I was trying to conduct research on liturgical music at a number of churches in the area, doing the bulk of my observations and interviews during the summers when I was not teaching. Once my son was firmly ensconced as a chanter, I decided to join him for an apprenticeship of my own, in a process that spanned several years. At first, I experienced a combination of reluctance and resentment. When the elderly head chanter indicated I should take a turn, I was reluctant to chant verses on my own because of my inexperience, and then resentful when other chanters intoned them with less musicality than I could have mustered. I was also hampered by my inability to read sheet music well, for while many chanters in Greece use Byzantine music notation, Greek-American churches now have abundant materials in Western notation. Here is where my own son became my teacher, guide, and key informant, because his sight-reading skills allowed him to flawlessly tackle any sheet music handed to him. Additionally, he had been doing a great deal of his own research on Greek Orthodox liturgical music, its system of eight musical modes or "tones" (*ihi*), and the structure and cycle of liturgical hymns and texts. While I, too, knew many of these things, his knowledge quickly outstripped mine: the only thing I still had over him was my fluency in Greek.

Our relationship at the chanter's stand was contentious for quite a while, because while I had parental authority over my son, I remained subordinate to him as a chanter, given his musical mastery. The priest and other parishioners heaped praise on his head (and rightly so), pointing out how much he was contributing at his young age. Meanwhile, my research was borne out of a lifetime of having witnessed women's voices being marginalized in the patriarchal context of Greek Orthodox liturgical practice, and I bristled at the same dynamic emerging between me and my own son. I frequently pointed out to him that all of his musical knowledge had come as a result of *my* labor, in paying for his piano lessons, not to mention all the housework I performed while he watched Byzantine chant videos on YouTube.

Gradually, however, as my own familiarity increased, I began to feel more competent at sight-reading the Orthros hymns, and gradually came to see the predictable patterns into which they fell, and to better understand their hymnal and musical cycles. I became more at ease with taking my turn at the stand, jumping in and even improvising when necessary. This is precisely the kind of apprenticeship I had longed to have while in the field on Skyros! From this position, I am coming to appreciate the role of a chanter within a church congregation, and especially to recognize the many spaces where women's voices can and do matter, and how younger men, like my son, think of the issues of gender and voice in a liturgy completely differently from older generations. We remain a comfortable team, and our current dynamic is an active collaboration. However, with the advent of COVID restrictions on church attendance and on choral singing as a "super spread" activity (Read 2020), the church was now restricted by the bishop to the use of one chanter, or two in the case of myself and my son, since we live together. During the summer of 2020, while he visited my parents out of state, I served as the sole chanter for all the services, which were attended by masked parishioners who spaced themselves out by six feet or more, and which were also livestreamed on social media. While such intense participation greatly increased my confidence and competence, I have still found myself "reporting" to my son on how I managed to execute a particularly long and melodically complex hymn. It seems that I remain an apprentice, looking to him for guidance.

CONCLUSION: FIELDWORK AS RELATIONSHIP

Fieldwork is transformative. It has the power to turn strangers into friends and friends back into strangers, and to turn mothers into apprentices to their own children, thereby shifting and complicating the power dynamics in the family. Why, then, did I feel like my doctoral training gave so little attention to the effects of such relationships? For example, I prepared for my preliminary doctoral exams by immersing myself in the scholarly literature related to my chosen specializations, including ethnographies of Greece, the anthropology of gender, and the ethnomusicology of Greece, the Balkans, and the Middle East. While I was fortunate to receive a seminar in ethnographic methods, it felt as though the emphasis was on the politics of ethnography, and to a lesser extent research techniques, rather on how we would operate day to day and on an emotional level in the field. Even more fortunately, I received support for a summer of field methods training, accompanying my then-advisor to her own field site in Montana, as well as a seminar in writing research proposals, and another on dissertation writing; again, all of these proved useful, but tended to downplay the emotional and relational realities I would confront while trying to gather "data." If my training was at all typical (which I'm fairly confident it was), then many, if not most, graduate students in anthropology go into the field less than adequately equipped to navigate the kinds of interpersonal relationships that fundamentally shape their research. Yes, we are admonished about romantic and sexual relationships in the field (and there is a growing body of literature on the subject, such as Markowitz and Ashkenazi 1999; and Rice 2019), and the subject of children in the field has been broached (Cassell 1987). Indeed, the ethnographic literature abounds with tales of the intimacies of friendship and fictive kinship as a factor in fieldwork (see, for example, Grindal and Salomone 1995; Kaufmann and Rabodoarimiadana 2003). So, too, has the notion of friendship in the field has been problematized, as Driessen (1998) points out. Yet my graduate training de-emphasized such topics, in favor of the theoretical contributions of such ethnographic fieldwork, informed as it surely was by such relationships.

Beyond our topical training, the overwhelmingly monastic nature of the traditional academy is also, I believe, fairly hostile to friendship, and certainly to family (ask any single mother with a PhD, or any tenure-track woman with children). Nevertheless, as graduate students, we do forge life-long friendships from among our cohorts. Yet we may also feel betrayed by these friendships, or at least mistrustful, when we are forced to compete with our friends for scarce resources, including our advisors' time, departmental awards, assistantships, fieldwork grants, and job opportunities. We thus set out into the field less than ideally prepared for how we will be received, or for the conditions under which we are expected to produce "results." We may lose sight of the central idea that *fieldwork is relationship*.

While no one on Skyros offered me the option of a fictive kin relationship (though they did say that they could "make a Skyrian" out of my son), it was also apparent that personal friendships were key to any progress I made, and that my ability to function in the field was dependent on how Skyrians interpreted my web of relations among friends and family members. Likewise, my current fieldwork on liturgical chanting would be greatly impoverished without the community's positive views of my son (and therefore of me), and without his role as my understanding and compassionate informant and guide. This is not unique only to my experience in the field, but common to all of us as anthropologists, wherever we find ourselves working. This is why I will continue to teach my students that any knowledge anthropologists have gained during fieldwork comes as a direct outgrowth of the relationships formed there, relationships that are never merely transactional, even though they may be complex, fraught, or fleeting.

REFERENCES

Abu-Lughod, Lila. 1991. "Writing against Culture." In *Recapturing Anthropology: Working in the Present*, edited by Richard Fox, 137–162. Santa Fe, CA: School of American Research Press.

Bargesian, Igor. 2000. "When Text becomes Field: Fieldwork in 'Transitional' Societies." In *Fieldwork Dilemmas: Anthropologists in Postsocialist States*, edited by H. G. DeSoto and N. Dudwick, 119–129. Madison, WI: University of Wisconsin Press.

Buchanan, Donna. 2006. *Performing Democracy: Bulgarian Music and Musicians in Transition*. Chicago: University of Chicago Press.

Cassell, Joan, ed. 1987. *Children in the Field: Anthropological Experiences*. Philadelphia, PA: Temple University Press.

Chianis, Sam. 2003. *Folk Songs of Skyros, Greece [Dhimotika Traghoudhia tis Skyrou]*. Volume with 4 accompanying CDs. Iraklio: Crete University Press.

Driessen, Henk. 1998. "The Notion of Friendship in Ethnographic Fieldwork." *Anthropological Journal on European Cultures*, 7(1): 43–62.

Faltaits, M. 2006. *Skyros* (3rd Historical Reprint). Translated by Mary McCallum. Paleopyrgos, Skyros: Manos Faltaits Museum.

Grindal, Bruce and Frank Salomone, eds. 1995. *Bridges to Humanity: Narratives on Anthropology and Friendship*. Prospect Heights: Waveland Press.

Gustafsson, Mai Lan. 2009. *War and Shadows: The Haunting of Viet Nam*. Ithaca, NY: Cornell University Press.

Hood, Mantle. 1960. "The Challenge of 'Bi-Musicality.'" *Ethnomusicology* 4(2): 55–59.

Kaufmann, J. and A. Rabodoarimiadana. 2003. "Making Kin of Historians and Anthropologists: Fictive Kinship in Fieldwork Methodology." *History in Africa*, 30: 179–194.

Kisliuk, Michelle. 1997. "(Un)doing Fieldwork: Sharing Songs, Sharing Lives." In *Shadows in the Field: New Perspectives for Fieldwork in Ethnomusicology*, edited by Gregory Barz and Timothy Cooley, 23–44. New York, NY: Oxford University Press.

Lambrou, Aliki. 2004. *Songs and Customs of Skyros [Traghoudhia ke Ethima tis Skyrou]*. Volume with 4 accompanying CDs. Skyros: Published by the Author.

Markowitz, Fran and Michael Ashkenazi, ed. 1999. Sex, Sexuality, and the Anthropologist. Urbana: University of Illinois Press. Montell, Lynwood. 1996. "Absorbed in Gospel Music." In *The World Observed: Reflections on the Fieldwork Process*, ed. Bruce Jackson & Edward Ives, pp. 118–127. Urbana: University of Illinois Press.

Narayan, Kirin. 1993. "How Native Is a 'Native' Anthropologist?" *American Anthropologist*, 95(3): 671–686.

Page, Helan. 1988. "Dialogic Principles of Interactive Learning in the Ethnographic Relationship." *Journal of Anthropological Research*, 44(2): 163–181.

Read, Richard. 2020. "Scientists to Choirs: Group Singing Can Spread the Coronavirus, Despite What CDC May Say." *Los Angeles Times*, June 1, 2020.

Rice, Kathleen. 2019. "Forbidden Fieldwork: The Affair as Research Method." *Anthropology and Humanism*, 44(2): 306–318.

Sugarman, Jane. 1997. *Engendering Song: Singing and Subjectivity at Prespa Albanian Weddings*. Chicago: University of Chicago Press.

Chapter 6

Friendships, Fieldwork, and the (De)Construction of Knowledge

Daniel Mains

This chapter is about the importance of friendship and maintaining relationships over long periods of time for anthropological research. Combining research and friendship necessarily involves a series of stumbles. I value my friends for their humor, kindness, and other qualities, but I also value them because collecting their experiences is an essential part of my work. Despite the struggles that are intrinsic to this dynamic, I have no doubts that friendships with the people I am studying are necessary for my work. Friendship enables connections between people in radically different circumstances. Friendship also enables a depth of understanding that can make traditional anthropological analysis very difficult.

I have known Desta and Afwerk since 2002 when I spent a summer in Jimma, Ethiopia studying Amharic and doing preliminary work for my PhD project. After that summer, a visit to the corner where they worked was always one of my first stops when I was in Jimma. In 2012 I was disappointed to find Desta gone. This was not so unusual. He sometimes took different odd jobs or simply disappeared from the corner for a few days. Afwerk told me that Desta was having problems, but did not elaborate. When I finally tracked Desta down he was chewing *chat* (a mild stimulant, sometimes called *khat*) at a cafe, what many chat chewers referred to as a morning "eye-opener" (*ehjebeneh* in Oromo). He told me he had not worked for five days. His wife left him for another man. She left all three of their children with him. "My mind is not right," he said.

In the ten years I had known Desta he had gone through ups and downs, but I had never seen him like this. "Now that my wife is gone who is going to look after the kids and cook while I work?" he asked. "I've been buying food from restaurants and tea houses for my kids. I can't work. I am too depressed. I've been selling my furniture for money to buy food." Desta had no family in the area that he could rely on. An additional worry was that his son was graduating from kindergarten and needed new clothes for the occasion. I offered to take him shopping. Although neither of us had much experience shopping for children's clothes, we eventually found the right spot and I bought an outfit for his son—clothes that he could wear to the graduation and still use for playing and running around the neighborhood.

In 2014 I had trouble finding Afwerk. I visited his corner a few times and heard different stories. Finally, someone told me that Afwerk had been ill and away from work for months. I visited him at his mother's house. He looked frail and weak. He wanted to go back to work, and was afraid of losing his customers, but it was clear to me that he was in no position to return to repairing bicycles anytime soon. I had 120 *birr* (about $6 in 2014) in my pocket and I gave it all to him. Since I was only in town for a few days and needed to leave early the next morning, I worried that I would not see Afwerk again.

These were not typical encounters with Desta and Afwerk. Usually I would wander to their corner and pull up a stool to chat while they worked. One of us would invite the other for coffee and whether it had been two days or two years since we had last spoke the conversation was easy and full of humor. They had many changes in their lives, but I knew both for at least ten years before they experienced something like a crisis that completely destabilized their lives. The work that had been a constant for so many years was disrupted. Not only was the long-term future uncertain, but survival in the immediate present was threatened. As a researcher, I found crises such as these fascinating. After both of these encounters I returned to my hotel room and wrote up notes on our conversation, shaken by their struggles but still documenting. It was because of our long-term friendship that I learned about these dramatic changes in their lives. These crises, however, also demonstrated the limits of our friendship. It was painful for me to learn about Afwerk and Desta's struggles, but in both cases I quickly departed, flying far from Jimma and any obligations I might have to help. As Desta liked to joke, I move between the United States and Ethiopia like he travels from Jimma to Serbo—a town twenty kilometers away. During my brief visits to Jimma I was able to do little more than give them small amounts of money, which was certainly appreciated, but did not solve their problems.

Textbooks on anthropological research methods rarely discuss friendship—the term does not appear in the index of H. Russell Bernard's more than 700 page classic—*Research Methods in Anthropology*. Perhaps this is because it is extremely difficult to provide prescriptive advice about friendship and research. In some ways, Lisa Tillmann-Healy's (2003) admirable attempt to articulate how to use friendship as a method demonstrates just how difficult it is to teach someone how to make friends and combine friendship with research. The best that I can offer are stories about my experiences.

I love talking about Afwerk and Desta in the classroom, particularly their ingenuity in making a living as bicycle mechanics. I usually save the stories that I tell in this chapter for particular moments when I want to convey the complexity of fieldwork. These are stories about the ambiguities of fieldwork, how I got to know two people very well, my struggle to maintain these relationships, and what I learned with the passage of time. When I tell these stories to students, I do not necessarily have a definite lesson I want to impart. Rather, these stories are reflections on the risks and rewards of combining friendship and long-term research.

BEGINNINGS—SUMMER 2002

The sun was shining and the air was moist after a heavy rain. I had only been in Jimma a couple days and was still trying to get my bearings. The mud in the alley by my hotel had dried enough that I could take a shortcut to the main road. The point where the dirt alley hit the asphalt was a jumble of economic activity—a woman selling papayas, two tailors operating pedal-powered sewing machines, a man selling bundles of chat, and two bicycle repairmen. All were taking advantage of the space afforded by the alley to set up shop on this busy asphalt road near Jimma's bus station. But on this first visit none of this registered. There was too much stimulus to absorb. All eyes were on me as I emerged from the alley. There were few foreigners in Jimma and even fewer who took short cuts through alleys. I shouted a good morning to everyone in Amharic and immediately the two bicycle repairmen were on their feet, walking my way for a handshake and an introduction. Desta was the first to shake my hand, a huge smile stretching across his face. My anxiety immediately melted. Afwerk was slightly slower to open up but once we were talking the layers of conversation became deeper and deeper. Perhaps because Amharic was not a first language for either of them, they were surprisingly patient with my limited linguistic capabilities. We exchanged names and I gave them my basic story—from the United States, an anthropology student, intent on learning Amharic and studying Jimma's history, planning to stay for six weeks.

After that, I made a point of passing by the corner where the alley met the asphalt as much as possible. Afwerk and Desta never failed to greet me. Usually I accepted their offer of a wooden stool and sat down to visit. By the end of my six weeks I felt that we were friends. I wanted them to like me and it seemed that they felt the same. The hardest part of field research for me is approaching new people, but Afwerk and Desta always made me feel welcome. I gradually got to know the others who made their living on the corner—a young man who ran a video house, a barber, a honey seller across the street. There was also the unemployed young man who had recently returned from fighting in the Eritrea/Ethiopia war, energetic secondary school students who frequently rented bikes, and various others, usually men, who stopped off to share chat and cigarettes with Afwerk and Desta. For me, the corner was a site of great comfort. At the end of my visit I snapped a few photos of Afwerk and Desta and the gang that hung around the corner—a small crowd of young men posing on the sidewalk with arms slung over shoulders. I mailed copies from the United States, and these photos eventually made it into the albums that I perused when I later visited Desta and Afwerk at their homes.

OCTOBER 2003—BACK TO JIMMA

I had been back in Jimma for less than two weeks before Desta invited me to his house. It was a short walk from the corner where he worked, in a neighborhood filled with cheap rentals for day laborers. Desta's house was a single room—half of the only building in a large plot bordered by a fence. Sugarcane filled the edges of the compound and a muddy stream flowed through one corner of the property. We did not stay long, just enough time for Desta to introduce me to his wife and some of the young people who were hanging out at his place. The house was newly constructed—dirt floors, unfinished dirt walls, no ceiling dividing the rafters and tin roof from the rest of the house, and no electricity. Desta's room was filled with the high quality wooden furniture that is made in Jimma's many carpentry shops. With so much furniture there was almost no open space in the room. "Furniture is a savings plan," Desta said with a grin, "any money I spend on furniture cannot be lost on *tej* [honey wine] and *chat*."

I spent a lot of time with Desta over the next few weeks. He even helped me find an apartment to rent. But it quickly became clear to me that I was violating unwritten rules about behavior for someone of my nationality and status. I was the subject of insults as I walked down the street—"*duriye ferenj*"—a foreigner who engages in the rude behavior of young men. Another acquaintance took me aside to tell me that he was hearing rumors about me and that I should be careful who I spend time with. Initially I took this as a consequence of fieldwork—in order to do my research I had to interact with people from all walks of life. There were, however, a couple instances when young men in my neighborhood acted in a threatening manner toward me. I was still adjusting to life in Jimma and it was difficult to interpret precisely what was happening, so I responded by distancing myself from Desta and Afwerk. I still visited them frequently at their workplace, but we rarely spent time together outside of that. Desta often questioned why I never invited him to my home and he became a bit withdrawn during my visits. I told myself that I would be in Jimma for eighteen months, and there would be plenty of time to invite Desta over after I settled into things. As time passed he eventually became accustomed to the added distance in our relationship, and returned to his usual talkative self.

HISTORIES OF FRIENDSHIP AND WORK

My research project was centered on the experiences of urban youth, particularly unemployed school leavers and those working in the informal economy. I employed participant observation, a research method that is perhaps uniquely associated with anthropology. There are many forms of participation in daily life that do not require friendship, but it is absolutely essential for the kind of hanging out I was doing with unemployed youth and those working in the informal economy. A key aspect of friendship is the feeling that one is welcome. I always felt a low level of anxiety before joining a group of *chat* chewing unemployed youth or sitting down with young men as they worked. Friendship erased that feeling, I knew my friends were happy to see me. It would have been extremely awkward to sit for hours talking with people with whom I felt no connection. My unstructured research was, therefore, necessarily spent with friends.

I was nearly a year into my research before I sat down with Afwerk for a formal interview about his life history. There are limits to what can be learned through observation and casual interaction. I wanted to ask him more specific questions about his past and his desires for the future. I also wanted to collect information on his income, expenses, social network, and attitudes about work and status. If friendship eases participant observation, it can make these more formal and structured dimensions of research slightly awkward. Sharing one's daily income and expenses is not a typical dimension of friendship, and unlike our previous interactions this one was largely one-sided—I asked the questions and they answered. I arranged a series of four weekly meetings with Afwerk, similar to ones I organized with a number of other young men. I paid Afwerk 250 *birr* (around $30) for his time, the same as I offered to others who participated in this more intensive phase of my research. My thought was that 250 *birr* was enough money to be useful, but not enough for crowds of youth to demand to be involved in my research. Aside from buying each other tea and coffee, this was my first economic exchange with Afwerk. I worried that it might disrupt our relationship, but it did not. Money and research participation were exchanged without any noticeable change in our friendship. Perhaps the ease with which this interaction occurred demonstrates the limits of our friendship. I was still an outsider, significant differences in power separated us, and this made it possible to incorporate formal data collection into our relationship.

I often peppered Afwerk with questions as he worked, but now with an audio recorder on the table I began asking about his life history. Desta taught Afwerk to fix bicycles around the year 2000 when Afwerk was twenty years old, but Desta and Afwerk had been friends long before this. They lived in the same neighborhood and their families knew each other. In their younger years, they worked together as shoeshines and for a time Desta stayed with Afwerk at his mother's house to escape from family turmoil. Before becoming a bicycle mechanic Afwerk had been working at the bus station, escorting passengers to hotels for a small commission from hotel managers. Afwerk had a falling out with the bus station manager and was banned from the station. He knew Desta had been making decent money fixing bicycles and it did not take long for him to learn the basic skills and save the money to purchase the tools he needed to work.

Even before becoming friends Desta and Afwerk led similar lives. Afwerk dropped out of school in grade seven after struggling to pass his courses. He tried doing some carpentry but quickly gave this up for "*duriyenet*," the life of a *duriye*, in this case meaning living on and off the streets and making a living from petty theft and odd jobs. "It's not a bad life. It was fun to have money. I would just move from town to town and enjoy life as long as the money was there. If I ran out of money I could always sell my shoes or borrow from a friend."

Eventually at the age of sixteen or seventeen Afwerk tired of street life and moved back in with his mother and started working as a shoeshine. It was very difficult to reestablish relationships with his family and neighbors. "The kids in the neighborhood were afraid of me because I had forced them to give me money. Eventually they saw that my behavior had changed. I was not staying out at night or drinking heavily. People were surprised by my change. They slowly began to trust me again."

Desta moved to Jimma from the Kaffa region with his parents when he was a child, around five years old. His parents split up shortly after arriving in Jimma and his mother left for a small town near Asandabo. This was around 1984, the height of Ethiopia's famine and times were tough for many families. Desta's father left to fight as a government soldier in the civil war that was raging in the northern part of the country. Desta initially lived with extended family, but it wasn't long before he moved out and joined the many other kids who were living on the streets.

Desta spent many years working around the bus station, carrying loads and anything else he could do for money.

"I liked living on the streets," he explained, "I liked sleeping outside instead of inside. I like the chewing *chat*, smoking cigarettes, and especially all of the talk and action. Once I hitchhiked to Addis Ababa and stayed for a week, just to check out the scene. The kids there told me to go back to Jimma, life is not easy in Addis. But you get tired of this sort of life. You learn the difference between right and wrong and between people and animals. Sometimes I go back to those sidewalks and verandas where I used to sleep just to see it again. I always go alone and it gives me a powerful feeling. The kids today who are living on the streets are much tougher than I ever was."

This narrative comes from an interview I conducted with Desta in 2004, after we had gotten to know each other quite well.

During this interview Desta told me another story to explain his transition from living on the streets to a more settled life.

I was gambling and I won thirty *birr*. I was still young and a group of bigger, older boys surrounded me and demanded that I give them the money. I refused and one of them kicked me in the back. He kicked me so hard that he broke my spine. I slept on the street that night. The next day someone took me to the free Mother Theresa clinic. I was surrounded by other patients who were sick and dying. Someone would die every day. I prayed to God that I would be healed and the boy who kicked me would die. At that time I was not very religious, but I kept praying and eventually I healed. Later I heard that the boy who kicked me contracted a skin disease that killed him. That I could survive and he should die is obviously God's work. Everything is in God's hands.

It was not long after this that Desta began working as a shoeshine and left the streets to live with Afwerk's family. Desta began selling lottery tickets on the street and earned enough money to rent a room of his own. He bought tools and taught himself to fix bikes. Before long he owned a small fleet of bicycles that generated money as rentals.

WORKING AND GROWING A FAMILY

The late 1990s and early 2000s were a good time to be operating a bicycle repair and rental business in Jimma. The city was large and had enough paved roads that bicycles were very useful. There was not a lot of competing traffic from other vehicles and public transportation was not available on many inner-city routes. Bicycles offered a low-cost alternative to walking. Desta gradually built up his business and by 2001 he owned eight cycles that he rented, had 2,800 *birr* in the bank, and was earning 40—50 *birr*/day (about 8 *birr*/USD at the time). This prosperity did not last. He began having trouble with stolen bicycles. At one point he lent 800 *birr* to his step-father and the money was never returned. By 2003, his daily income was down to 10–20 *birr*.

It was amid this financial turmoil that Desta met his first wife.

> I was depressed and drinking heavily every night, buying drinks for my friends too. She advised me to stop wasting money. She had a bicycle and I had lots of furniture. We decided to live together. I could rent out her bicycle and I could save money by eating my meals at home. I still don't make a lot of money but I have been saving and purchasing cycles again.

In May 2004 Afwerk told me that Desta's wife gave birth to a son and I suggested to Desta that I come to his house to photograph his child. He was living in an outlying neighborhood. "It is much better here," he told me, "there is no place where I can go out at night and spend money drinking." I met Desta at his corner late in the afternoon and we walked together to his house, stopping along the way to buy a few small things for his wife. As usual, Desta was happy and talkative. He shouted greetings to everyone we saw, drawing attention to my presence, and noting that I once sent him seven photos from America.

In terms of family and finances Afwerk's life was much more stable. He lived with his mother and sisters and expressed little interest in a place of his own. Afwerk's mother earned money cleaning houses and baking *injera* for other families. One of his sisters worked as a cleaner at Jimma University—a stable and relatively well-paid job. She covered many of the household expenses for Afwerk's family.

In 2008 I was back in Jimma for the first time since finishing my fieldwork in 2005. I had finished my PhD, married, had a child, and published my first article based on my research on young men in Jimma. Afwerk and I went to Desta's house to greet his wife and meet his new son. He had moved into a new house, in the same neighborhood but even further from the city center and the nearest asphalt road. This time he owned the land and paid for the construction of the house himself. His two rooms were packed with even more wooden furniture than before. Desta was particularly excited about a large color television and DVD player. "The kids from the neighborhood all come over to my house to watch television," he boasted. He put on a DVD about the life of Jesus for us to watch as we visited and drank the fresh coffee that Desta's wife prepared. It was a happy visit with lots of joking about families and children. On the walk back to town Desta insisted that we stop at St. Michael's church. He showed me around and emphasized that he spends a great deal of time at the church. When I visited Desta's house again in 2009 his family had grown further and he had a daughter in addition to the two sons. The older of the two sons was attending a private Catholic kindergarten. Despite the challenges of work, Desta's family was growing and his life was becoming more stable and comfortable.

STRUGGLES WITH GIFTS AND FIELD WORK

As an anthropologist who writes and teaches about gift exchange (Mains 2012, 2013), I should probably be better at giving gifts. Particularly on my initial return trips after finishing long-term fieldwork in 2005, I felt that I needed to get gifts for most of the young men who were involved in my research. In 2009 a day or two before departing for Ethiopia I went to a tourist shop in St. Louis, where I was living at the time, and bought what can only be described as a bunch of crap: St. Louis themed shot glasses, playing cards, and other things like this. I gave Afwerk a shot glass with a picture of the St. Louis Arch on it.

The 2009 visit to Desta's house was not pleasant. I had to work hard to talk Afwerk into coming and promised to pay him for the time he missed from work. Such economic demands were totally out of character for Afwerk. He was grouchy the whole time and the conversation, the *chewata* (play), never really flowed. Later that evening, back at my hotel I got a call from Afwerk on my mobile phone. Afwerk drank heavily every evening, and he had never called me at night. He was angry. He told me that our friendship was over and that I should not bother trying to speak with him again. He blamed it on the shot glass. "Do you think I am a drunkard?!" After hanging up I felt sick. It did not feel good to lose a friend. I flashed back to all of the times I had joked with the guys who hang around Afwerk's corner about his drinking. "If drinking honey wine was an Olympic event, Afwerk would win a gold medal." Things like this would always draw a laugh from the crowd, but thinking back it was clear that Afwerk was not laughing. He enjoyed joking about honey wine and did not hide the fact that he drank every night, but he was not happy to be the object of the joke.

Friendship depends on trust. Each party must trust affection exists between them. For the most part, that trust does not need to be questioned and this creates a sense of comfort. Friends can enjoy the feeling that they are liked and appreciated. My gift violated that sense of trust, implying that I was mocking Afwerk, thinking poorly of him. Such a gift between acquaintances would probably quickly be forgotten, but between friends it called a long relationship into question.

I did not sleep well for the next week as I thought through everything I had done to destroy my relationship with Afwerk. I tried to talk with him and apologize but he was not having it. Then, about a week after the incident I got a call from him. He apologized and invited me to his mother's house for dinner. Although their house was in the centrally located neighborhood where I rented a room while doing my long-term fieldwork in Jimma, it was my first time visiting. Afwerk's mother served us simple but delicious lentils and injera (the soft spongey bread that is the staple food in highland Ethiopia), and we looked through family photo albums. In my experience looking at photo albums is a must when visiting friends in Ethiopia, but Afwerk's photos were unique. He always wore dusty coveralls while working on bikes that hid his flair for fashion. I was amazed to see photo after photo of him in different outfits and styles—three-piece suits, denim, and a full suit of camouflage topped with a beret. He also had a number of photos of himself with his dog, "Hard." Afwerk is the only person in Jimma I have ever observed walking his dog.

In the end, I made up for the thoughtless shot glass gift by buying Afwerk two sets of pliers and a spoke wrench. He was pleased, explaining that if I had just given him money it would disappear, but these tools would help him earn an income long into the future. By this point in our relationship I should have known that Afwerk takes gifts seriously. When I left Jimma in 2005 after completing eighteen months of fieldwork many of the young men involved in my research stopped by my house with small parting gifts for me. The gifts were thoughtful but usually quite similar—I ended up with four identical wall hangings depicting traditional Ethiopian music instruments. Afwerk's gift was, of course, unique. It was a wig, made from the skin and fur of a colobus monkey, traditionally worn by Oromo warriors. Between 2005 and 2011 I moved seven times and each time that wig was carefully packed and found a place of honor in my new home. When I see Afwerk he often asks if I still have the wig and he is always happy to hear that it is still on display and that I use it as an excuse to tell visitors about him.

Marina de Regt (2015, 2019) has thoughtfully explored the relationship between friendship, fieldwork, and reciprocity. Particularly given the massive inequalities that often exist between western anthropologists and the people they study, friendships frequently involve tensions over money and reciprocity. I have argued elsewhere (Mains 2013) that among young men in urban Ethiopia it is impossible to separate friendship and money. Friendship implies a willingness to provide help when it is needed. In contrast to many of the young men involved in my research, Afwerk never asked me for financial support. Gifts were important for our relationship, but more for their symbolic value than their economic utility. As de Regt (2015, 2019) explains, it can be very difficult to maintain mutually satisfactory relations of reciprocity in friendships between anthropologists and research participants, but in the cases of Afwerk and Desta I never felt that monetary support was a fundamental aspect of our relationship.

I was fortunate that things worked out with Afwerk. I do not know what made his anger subside. It is unlikely that he would have become so upset if not for the depth of our relationship. Close interactions over many years bring opportunities for friction. As I get to know people I have a tendency to gently mock and joke about certain characteristics that I actually appreciate. I know little about the details of Afwerk's nightly honey wine drinking. Afwerk and I were stumbling through a long-term friendship, one not made any easier by the immense spatial and economic distance between us.

Over the years Afwerk and Desta's friendship with each other also shifted. Although for many years they continued to work on the same corner, Desta gradually moved further down the street and conversations between them more or less disappeared. One would sometimes gossip to me about the other. There was definitely friction between them and I did my best to stay out of this—my relationship with each of them was complicated enough as it was. My sense is that they continue to have genuine concern for each other, but their day-to-day interactions are minimal.

FALLING APART AND COMING TOGETHER

In 2015 Afwerk had miraculously recovered from his illness, perhaps he was a bit thinner than in years past, but he was certainly healthy. In the year since I had last seen him he had spent two months at an Orthodox Christian Church in Addis Ababa, taking a holy water cure. He had also spent a few days at a church in Menz, a full day's journey from Addis, also for the holy water. When I asked him for more details about his health he simply smiled and used the English "mental case" to describe his problem and said that he was better now. Afwerk credited prayer and holy water for his recovery, but it is unclear what he would have done without his mother and sisters. He had no savings to support himself for the months when he was not working. I assume that his sisters paid for his travels to churches in Addis and Menz. He said nothing to me about support from his mother and sisters, but it is clear that they were essential for his survival.

The chaos in Desta's life when we last met in 2012 had subsided. After selling nearly all of his furniture to get by after his wife left him, Desta pulled himself together. He found a new wife and started working again. The new wife embraced his children and when we met in 2015 she had just given birth to a child fathered by Desta. He had sold his house and built a new home on a plot of land very close to Boye Swamp, at the edge of the city, an area that had still not been incorporated into the formal city plan.

Desta was doing better, but he was still very concerned about his ten-year-old son. Desta took me aside, away from the people who hung around his workplace to explain that in the turmoil of the days following his wife's departure, his son left the house.

> He is a *duriye*. He sleeps on the street. If he wants to be a *duriye* and hang out on the streets during the day I can live with that, but I can't have him sleeping on the streets. This is too stressful for me. Sometimes I see him, but he always runs and hides before I can talk to him . . . You know, when my wife left it was with one of my friends, this made it even worse. I felt terrible, I was almost crazy. I was buying food at restaurants and then running it home for the kids. I could not work. I sold almost everything I owned. Now prices have gone up and it is impossible to buy everything again. I am like a snake that looks like it is dead, but it is just shedding its skin. That's how I feel, like I have been reborn after shedding my skin, like I have returned from the dead.

Before leaving I gave Desta money to help with his family. He later showed me a photo that his new wife took of their baby son laying on a blanket surrounded with the 100 *birr* notes I gave him.

In 2017 I visited Desta's house for dinner. On entering I immediately noticed that the furnishing consisted of the foam floor mattresses (*ferash*) that are common in Muslim households and there were posters of Muslim religious art on the wall. When Desta tuned the television to a Quranic education program, I asked if he had become a Muslim and he laughed at my surprise and then explained,

> My wife is a Muslim. After things fell apart with my first wife I could not be a Christian anymore. At my previous house most of my neighbors were Christian. We had a good relationship, but when things went bad for me they disappeared. My new neighbors are Muslim and they have treated me like family. Islam is also good because it prevents me from wasting money on alcohol. Muslims are moral people. I am still the same. Before I was Desta, now I am Desta. But now Islam is better for me.

Desta continuously praised his new wife.

> She is from Addis Ababa and she worked for two years in the Middle East. Her family has money and she was still willing to marry me and take care of my children. She is amazing. She believes in me. She has faith that our poverty will pass and that I can earn money and succeed. I felt bad because I had sold my old television and had no money for a new one, but she encouraged me to start saving. It did not take long before I bought a new television. It was the same

with our house. It started as two rooms, but she encouraged me to save and now we have three. She is very brave.

In my book on urban youth, based on research conducted before Desta's wife left him, I used Desta's story to demonstrate the possibility of building a family through precarious work (Mains 2012). Many young men who participated in my research in the early 2000s claimed that it was extremely difficult to fulfill the masculine norms of marriage and children. Desta demonstrated that in fact marriage and children were possible through self-employment, and that other young men not only wanted a family, but a particular type of family—for example, they consistently stressed the importance of offering one's children a private education. My friendship with Desta allowed me to see twists and turns in his life that complicated my earlier conclusions. After his first wife left him Desta's family completely fell apart. He had no means of working and looking after his children. With the help of his new wife Desta's family is once again on stable ground, and his oldest son is no longer living on the streets. Marriage and raising a family were possible for Desta, but his situation was extremely precarious. He had no family member he could turn to for help. Relationships with neighbors that appeared useful dissolved with Desta's marriage. Given Desta's history of engagement in the Orthodox church, the shift to Islam could not have been as simple as he described. Changing religions must have been stressful, but not as stressful as living without a woman to raise his children.

In 2017, I ran into Afwerk as he was coming out of a honey wine bar in the early afternoon. He was in a fine mood and we walked together to his workplace where he bought me a hot glass of ginger tea. His body had visibly changed. For the first time in the fifteen years that I had known him he had a stocky, muscular build. He explained that he had given up chewing chat and smoking cigarettes and was now exercising in the mornings at the nearby stadium.

When I commented that his new workplace is connected by a newly paved road to his mother's house he surprised me by stating that he no longer lived there. Typical of Afwerk and many Ethiopians, his answers to my surprised questions were brief and indirect. Me: "Why did you move out?" Afwerk: "Isn't it better?" Me: "Where are you staying?" Afwerk: "Around . . . Out." Eventually he told me, "I've married and I am renting a place in the city center with my wife." It was so surprising that I made him repeat himself to be sure that I had not misunderstood. "This time don't buy me tools," he said, "We need to celebrate. Let's drink beer and eat *tibs* [fried meat]."

I share Afwerk's love for drink and good times, but I had never had a beer or honey wine with him. I had felt a need to maintain a sort of professional distance during my early research. Unfortunately, I came down with a bit of food poisoning the night before our date, but I ate some pepto bismol and managed to meet Afwerk and his wife at the appointed time. Afwerk wore a rakish cap and his wife was wrapped in a white cotton shawl—traditional formal wear for women in much of Ethiopia. We drank big bottles of cold lager and ate fried strips of beef dipped in a spicy pepper sauce. I updated Afwerk about my children and extended family—he always asked about my sister Sara who he had met once. I described the bicycle I use for commuting in the United States and my recent bike accident that was a result of too many drinks and recklessly riding at night.

It was quickly clear that Afwerk had found a good match in his wife, as she was equally adept in the sort of joking conversation (*chewata*) in which Afwerk excelled. She had moved to Jimma from the Wolayta region ten years ago. While Afwerk teased her because she had never gone to school, she came right back at him, noting that because he had always lived with his mother, he knew nothing about cooking or managing a house.

Near the end of our dinner Afwerk remarked that I would now have something new to write about when I returned to the United States. I could tell another chapter in the story of his life. I have written about Afwerk before, he is one of the case studies of young men working in the informal economy that I used in my book, but I have never directly shared my writing with him. A marriage is a common narrative device for ending stories, but if there is anything I have learned from following the lives of Afwerk and Desta, it is that there is no ending and no beginning. There are milestones like marriage, divorce, childbirth, and disagreements with friends but life continues. The moments of conversation and passing time are just as important as anything else.

CONCLUSION

Although it is common for anthropologists to reflect on how they are positioned in relation to their research, these reflections are generally brief and are rarely included in journal articles. Anthropologists do not often pull back the curtain to describe the actual process of making connections with others that are necessary for fieldwork. An important exception is the 1995 volume *Bridges to Humanity: Narratives on Anthropology and Friendship*, edited by Bruce Grindal and Frank Salamone. *Bridges to Humanity* offers fascinating essays on the complexities of friendship for conducting research, and how researchers' struggles to be liked by the people they study shape the construction of knowledge. As the title implies, many of these essays treat friendship as a means of making connections between people who live very different lives. Friendship is an ambiguous relationship, it is not marked by legal commitments and this ambiguity can create tensions when people are uncertain that a friendship exists.

The preface to *Bridges to Humanity* references the origins of the journal *Anthropology and Humanism* and this is where many discussions of fieldwork and friendship have been published (Taggert and Sandstrom 2011). Particularly interesting is Paloma Gay y Blasco and Liria de la Cruz Hernández's (2012) collaborative exploration of friendship and research. In this article anthropologist and research subject reflect on their relationship and the production of knowledge. De la Cruz Hernández's voice adds a great deal of depth to the discussion—like much of the writing on friendship, my analysis above does little to explain what Afwerk and Desta thought about me. Gay y Blasco (2017) followed up on this article five years later to explore the challenges of co-writing and finding an audience for the "reciprocal life story" she is producing with de la Cruz Hernández.

Friendship is a powerful tool in anthropological research. It is through friendship that I have come to better understand people like Afwerk and Desta who have lives completely different than mine. Over the years during my brief visits to Jimma I have increasingly spent more of my time with friends because we can reconnect so quickly. Friendship, however, also has the potential to undermine certain elements of anthropological knowledge production. It is common practice for anthropologists to take bits and pieces of people's lives and weave them together to support a theoretical argument, and that is certainly what I have done in my work. I have used parts of Afwerk and Desta's lives to bolster specific claims that I want to advance. I stand by those arguments, but even the relatively short descriptions I have provided here demonstrate that the process of reducing a life to evidence for a theoretical claim involves a high level of simplification. Afwerk's and Desta's lives are far more complicated than the arguments I have advanced, so complex that they are difficult to reduce to generalizable claims. But why tell a story if there is nothing that can be learned from it? Afwerk's response to this question appears to be similar to my own. He suggests that I would want to tell his story, including his recent marriage, without regard for its significance in generating theory. There is, however, little value for this type of story in academic anthropology. Afwerk is interesting for me because he has led a complex life, one far more precarious than my own and many of my readers, but perhaps not a life so different than millions of others who live in cities in the global south. It is a life that I only came to know through a long and tumultuous friendship. I could not have followed the complex turns in Afwerk and Desta's lives without maintaining a friendship—a friendship that was at times threatened by doubts and mistrust. But now that I have come to know Afwerk and Desta in such depth, I am reluctant to write about them again, at least not in the style that is typical for academic journals.

Perhaps friendship and research function together to create a cycle of creative destruction. Friendship generates knowledge, but with time the accumulation of depth, complexity, and detail destroys the possibility of fitting lives into neat categories of analysis. Close relationships and long-term fieldwork have a tendency to unsettle representational methodologies (Vannini 2015). Rather than producing generalized knowledge, the anthropologist is left with the task of describing lived experiences and narratives (Jackson 2013, 2017). This is the first time I have written about Afwerk and Desta in many years and I wonder if I will write about them again.

REFERENCES

Bernard, H. Russell. 2002. *Research Methods in Anthropology: Qualitative and Quantitative Approaches*, Third Edition. Walnut Creek: Altamira Press.

de Regt, Marina. 2015. "Noura and Me: Friendship as Method in Times of Crisis." *Urban Anthropology*, 44(1, 2): 43–70.

de Regt, Marina. 2019. "'In Friendship One Does Not Do Such Things': Friendship and Money in War-Torn Yemen." *Etnofoor*, 31(1): 99–112.

Gay y Blasco, Paloma and Liria de la Cruz Hernández. 2012. "Friendship, Anthropology." *Anthropology and Humanism*, 37(1): 1–14.

Gay y Blasco, Paloma. 2017. "Doubts, Compromises, and Ideals: Attempting a Reciprocal Life Story." *Anthropology and Humanism*, 41(1): 91–108.

Grindal, Bruce and Frank Salamone. 1995. *Bridges to Humanity: Narratives on Anthropology and Friendship*. Prospect Heights: Waveland Press.

Jackson, Michael. 2013. *The Wherewithal of Life: Ethics, Migration, and the Question of Wellbeing*. Berkeley, CA: University of California Press.

Jackson, Michael. 2017. *How Lifeworlds Work: Emotionality, Sociality, and the Ambiguity of Being*. Chicago, IL: University of Chicago Press.

Mains, Daniel. 2012. *Hope Is Cut: Youth, Unemployment, and the Future in Urban Ethiopia*. Philadelphia, PA: Temple University Press.

Mains, Daniel. 2013. "Friends and Money: Balancing Affection and Reciprocity among Young Men in Urban Ethiopia." *American Ethnologist*, 40(2): 335–346.

Taggert, James and Alan Sandstrom. 2011. "Introduction to "Long-Term Fieldwork." *Anthropology and Humanism*, 36(1): 1–6.

Tillmann-Healy, Lisa. 2003. "Friendship as Method." *Qualitative Inquiry*, 9(5): 729–749.

Vannini, Phillip, ed. 2015. *Non-Representational Methodologies*. New York, NY: Routledge.

Chapter 7

Staying in the Field

Living Arrangements, Violence, and the Female Anthropologist

Denielle Elliott

Where[1] we live during ethnographic fieldwork is tied to not only to our claims of expertise but also to how we know what we know in anthropology (Clifford 1983; Gupta and Ferguson 1997). Ethnographic fieldwork is as Allaine Cerwonka and Lisa Mallki (2007) explain fundamentally place-based, intuitive, sensed, and embodied. As ethnographers, we explore and come to understand everyday lives and public phenomena through methods that are intimate, social, and embodied. As Liisa Malkki writes, anthropology's claims are made based on "situated, long term, empirical field research" (2007, 164). Anthropologists carefully consider where they will live in the field because the decision is tied to methodology, epistemology, ethnographic authority, our complicities in larger power structures, in addition to safety and the limits of our financial resources (certainly for graduate students) (Clifford 1983; Marshall 1993). Where we live (at home or in the field) can also reflect our political values. Where we choose to live during fieldwork has unintended and unpredictable consequences not only for our research but also on ourselves as emplaced anthropologists (for instance think of the historical work of Jean Briggs (1971) and Napoleon Chagnon (1997)). The decision is as much ethical as it is methodological. Given how critical our living arrangements are then to ethnographic fieldwork, it is puzzling that more has not been written on it within anthropology.

We find good-enough accommodations that seem secure, take precautions to be safe in sometimes dangerous spaces, but we must balance these with working to be part of the communities we are going to live and work. The discipline of anthropology has historic, if often unsaid, rules that govern where and how we live during our ethnographic research that force us to

contend with how we balance questions of safety with political commitments to addressing racial discrimination, economic inequalities, and hetero-
normative and patriarchal ideas about women (in work, study, and life). It is
a fine balance that often makes itself most noticeable as we attempt to sort
our living arrangements in the field. How do we find safe housing but also be
a part of the communities we study? How do we maintain safety to body and
mind when we work in fieldsites rife with economic and political inequalities? What does it mean to ethically negotiate the gendered landscapes of
fieldsites? These questions are often left unanswered in anthropology methodology courses and we are left to fumble our way through. In this chapter,
I reflect on my own experiences of trying to navigate safety and security and
a violent encounter that happened during postdoctoral fieldwork in 2009. (I
describe in a fair amount of detail the attack and so some readers may not
want to read past page 102.)

Over the past twenty years, there have been increasing accounts by anthropologists who have talked about questions of safety, violence, and tensions
in fieldwork encounters. Cynthia Mahmood has written about her experience
of being assaulted and raped during fieldwork (2008), as did Eva Morena
(1995) and Alix Johnson (2016). There are also a number of edited volumes
that speak to fieldwork in violent contexts (Nordstrom and Robben 1995;
Ghassem-Fachandi 2009; Koonings, Kruijt, and Rodgers 2019; Lee 1994),
or to ethnographic fieldsites that raise other ethical, moral, and political tensions (Armbruster and Lærke 2010; Kulick and Wilson 1995). Such papers
and collections have highlighted how important it is for us to think about
encounters with violence in the field since ethnography is relational and our
knowledge co-created and dialogical (Fabian 1983; 2007). As Dara Culhane
writes, "Ethnographic knowledge emerges not through detached observation
but through conversations and exchanges of many kinds among people interacting in diverse zones of entanglement" (2017, 3). What we know emerges
through interaction (Fabian 2007) and we produce embodied accounts; and
thus, if the field includes violence or violent encounters, we must reflect critically on how that shapes our findings and conclusions.

I took up a postdoctoral position when I finished the PhD on a project
being led by a researcher at the London School of Hygiene and Tropical
Medicine (LSHTM) focusing on the very same sorts of questions I had
explored in Vancouver, but instead in western Kenya. The project aimed to
examine the "trial communities" that had emerged as a result of an AIDS
epidemic and the enormous amount of material and financial resources being
funneled into HIV/AIDS preventions and therapeutics. Kisumu county was
the site of dozens of clinical trials for everything from pre-exposure pro-
phylaxis to microbicides. Local Kenyans would lineup from 4:00 a.m. to
enroll in clinical trials offering honoraria for their participation. The trials

were well funded, drawing in millions of U.S. dollars, supporting Kenyans in all kinds of employment including as lead investigators, epidemiologists, statisticians, drivers, and security guards, in addition to many others.[2] The research project I joined aimed to study the everyday practices of these bioscientific enterprises, to better understand how Americans conduct research in East Africa.

These transnational medical research projects attracted many researchers and students from the United States, Canada, and Europe often with funding to pay expensive rates for rental housing. Like a tourist resort, cost of living increased, as did the demand for rental housing, exponentially in Kisumu as international HIV/AIDS researchers and program staff migrated to the city. I had never traveled to the African continent before. I arrived without any travel accommodations sorted. My postdoctoral supervisor said I would find something when I arrived, and I did: a little Kenyan hotel just two blocks from the main street. I stayed there for a couple of weeks until a Kenyan researcher with the U.S. Army's Walter Reed project found out, decided it was not a safe hotel, and arranged for me to stay in their guest house. As a non-American not affiliated with the Walter Reed project, I was asked to keep a low profile since it was generally reserved for Americans or those working with the U.S. Army. It was a lovely guesthouse, decadent by most standards, and I gained a sense of the comforts that American citizens working for the state department were used to while working in Kenya. For instance, my meals were prepared by a house cook, my room and laundry cleaned, and the yards maintained by a gardener. But it was a short-term solution only, and I had to find something else for the next year of research.

My LSHTM supervisor tried to persuade me and two other doctoral students working on the project that we should all rent a house together, a sort of project house, in the neighborhood of Millimani. Millimani is a neighborhood in Kisumu largely inhabited by Asians (wealthy Indian Kenyans who are business owners), wealthy Kenyans (elite politicians, business owners, and the odd scientist), and *wazungu* (Americans, Canadians, and Europeans). The houses are large, luxurious, and the yards landscaped with tropical plants and trees, usually staffed with an *askari* [guard], cleaning staff, and gardeners. I was uncomfortable with the idea of living in that neighborhood, and the three of us didn't want to live together either. Most of the Kenyans we were working with at the Kenya Medical Research Institute, the staff and research participants in the trials, did not live in Milimani (in fact, I can only think of one Kenya senior scientist that did at the time). Since my interest in the political economy of transnational clinical trials was in part fuelled by an interest in the ways in which these good-intentioned bioscientific interventions inadvertently increased inequities, it felt antithetical to me to live in a community where most of my Kenyan colleagues could not afford to live.

Figure 7.1   Typical Housing in Nyalenda, Kenya. *Source*: Provided by Denielle Elliott.

That said, it also seemed unrealistic to live in one of the many low-income settlements, like Nyalenda, where there was little infrastructure for safe and potable water, power, paved, or even gravel roads. Kenyans living in those areas frequently reported theft to me. My research materials would probably not be secure, and I would draw a lot of attention as a *mzungu* (singular version of *wazungu*). For a while I stayed in the neighborhood of Tom Mboya, adjacent to the medical research facilities where most of our ethnographies were being carried out. Owned by a South Asian family, it was a small compound with about five apartments and five small cottages. They were simple and sparse, and surrounded by gardens. It too was surrounded by a large stone wall and guarded by an *askari* at night. I rented a two-bedroom cottage, with a small kitchenette and bathroom. The other apartments and cottages were usually occupied by other solitary white women in Kisumu for research or studies on tropical or maternal health, agriculture, or forestry; once in a while a visiting religious fellow (usually Christian missionaries) would stay for a short term. I could walk to the research site within ten minutes. A Luo woman, Rachel, ran the place (hired by the owners) and she treated me like I was kin. I felt indebted regularly to her for helping me out with many things—where to find office supplies in town, who to call to get my bike repaired, where to buy local baskets. On the odd weekend, we'd travel to her home in Kakamega forest where her family lived. I'd drop her off and then go for a hike in the forest. This housing arrangement worked well for me for the first year.

Figure 7.2 The House on Lake Victoria. *Source*: Provided by Denielle Elliott.

But when I returned in 2009 to start a new research project, I wanted to find somewhere else to stay. There were issues at the compound: Rachel was increasingly unsatisfied with her work; and there were rumors that the owners were racist, treating the Kenyan staff poorly and not paying them adequate wages. I didn't want to seem complicit in their actions by staying there. Luckily a friend had a plot of land on the edge of Lake Victoria, just about 10 kms from town. He was building a simple home there and the property was currently vacant (he lived in the United States). At the time it didn't have power or running water but a well was being dug and a solar panel offered power. It also had a small kitchen with a fridge and gas stove, and a separate bathroom with a dry toilet and shower with hot water thanks to the solar power. The view was amazing—unobstructed lake views with fishermen, *kibokos* [hippopotamus], and endless species of birds. I had spent a lot of time there on weekends in 2007 and 2008, camping before structures were built, or just visiting for the day, heading out for a paddle in his kayaks. So when my friend offered the place for me to rent during my new postdoctoral project, I didn't think twice. His property was surrounded by a fishing village; most of whom were related to each other through marriage or blood. I could bike to my research site, the Lumumba hospital and site of the FACES (Family AIDS Care and Education Services) program, within thirty minutes along the dirt road, or if need be, I could catch a ride with a *piki piki* [motorbike] or *tuk tuk* [small motorized rickshaw].

When I told colleagues, other visiting researchers, and Kenyan friends that I was relocating to this lakeside paradise, many people raised questions about my safety. In fact, safety was a dominant theme among many living in Kisumu. In 2007, the year before the December elections, there was general unrest in Kenya, a sort of tension you could sense in the air. Mungiki, a religious sect or urban gang (depending on who you ask) that had evolved from Mau Mau, had been blamed for a series of vicious murders in Nairobi and other areas. In response, the police sought out suspected Mungiki members, arresting, assaulting, and killing many of them (Munene 2018). There were almost daily reports in the national newspapers of Mungiki related killings. In Kisumu, not far from our Tom Mboya guesthouse, we heard a series of gunshots one night. I was nervous; I had never lived anywhere where there was armed fighting. The next day the local news reported that a number of people had been shot and killed at another guesthouse. I was startled and brought it up with my postdoctoral supervisor, who initially dismissed my concerns. I think he assumed I was just a nervous Canadian woman getting upset about nothing. But details continued to emerge about what had happened over the following days. It wasn't a random attack; in fact, it was a police raid and the police had shot and killed almost everyone in the guesthouse. My supervisor reconsidered his position and asked me if I felt like I needed a gun. He could obtain a Glock for me from a Kenyan acquaintance. I couldn't tell if he was joking or not, but I declined.

Kenyan colleagues working on the clinical trials also reported being assaulted or robbed by assailants as they went home from work in the evenings, and their laptops and cellphones stolen. American colleagues working for large research studies had project housing to stay in, and those working with the U.S. Army or Centers for Disease Control and Prevention (CDC) had housing provided for them along with a long list of rules of what they were permitted to do while staying in Kenya. These rules were meant to ensure the safety of American citizens working abroad but many of the policies seemed to lack awareness of local cultural norms. For instance, some Americans could only take transportation with U.S. Embassy-approved vehicles (no taxis, no *tuk tuk*, or *piki piki*). U.S. Embassy employees that had long term contracts in Kisumu were provided with housing that had a large secure fence, Embassy-approved security guards, locking metal gates inside the house creating secure rooms, and often dogs (see Elliott 2014a for more details). It all felt like a rather exaggerated response to me; a response to fear rather than actual patterns of crime and violence.

Though 2007 and 2008 were particularly violent months for Kenyans due to the December 2007 national elections and the ethnic clashes that followed into 2008, for the most part Kenya is not what one might consider a "dangerous fieldsite" (Kovats-Bernat 2002; Nordstrom and Robben 2005). In fact, many nongovernmental organizations and corporations like Google have made it the East African headquarters because of its relative stability and security in sub-Saharan Africa. Every year, millions of tourists flock to Kenya to take safaris, go on birding tours, and simply enjoy the beaches of the coast. This is not to say it is without violence: carjackings, gun violence, and theft are all serious problems in Kenya, especially in Nairobi (jokingly referred to as "Nairobbery" in some tourist guide books).

When I started moving into the lakeside home of my friend, I considered these concerns for safety and tried to weigh them with how I hoped to conduct ethical, socially responsible fieldwork as a white Canadian in a place not my own. I considered dogs, considered local security guards, considered not needing any additional security. In the end, I decided to hire a night watchman, someone who came at dusk and left at dawn and kept watch on the property during the nights. The property also had a *fundi* [general caretaker and gardener] who lived on-site, so this strategy seemed more than enough. However, I didn't know how one went about hiring a security guard in Kenya, though many people had them. A friend who lived not far from this lakeside house also had a local night watchman and he offered to ask him for recommendations. Many of these local *askari* positions, largely untrained security guards, are filled by Maasai men who have migrated to urban centers in Kenya and Tanzania seeking paid employment (Munishi 2016). My friend, a respected senior Kenyan lawyer, and I arranged a meeting with his askari who would introduce us to another Maasai moran seeking work. That meeting went well, and we agreed on the terms of his employment (hours, salary, responsibilities) and his start date. In terms of methodological approaches to fieldwork, I thought trusting the recommendation of an esteemed Kenyan lawyer who knew the community, the level of risks, and the process for hiring a night watchman made sense, and I still believe this. But sometimes, no matter how much thought we put into trying to avoid dangerous situations in our fieldwork or lives, we find ourselves in the middle of it.

The construction wasn't quite finished at the lakeside house (the well was still being dug and the solar panel was yet to be installed), so I was slowly transitioning from the temporary guesthouse in town to the lake. That meant weekends at the lake and weekdays in town so Michael, the new night *askari*, started working weekends only. Michael spoke Maa, some Kiswahili, and no English. I spoke a little Dholuo, very little Kiswahili, and no Maa. Communication was challenging so we relied on whoever might be around to help translate. In advance of the position he asked for funds to buy a *rungu* [a wooden weapon for self-defence] and a spear, gear he deemed necessary to guard the lakeside property. He seemed pleasant enough. I ensured he had hot *chai* and biscuits each night, and he had access to the kitchen (a separate building from the main living and sleeping area).

In late February after he had been working for me for about three weeks, Michael arrived a bit early one Friday night. I was having dinner with a colleague, Robert (Bob) Bailey, from the University of Illinois-Chicago in the *banda* [shaded outdoor sitting area]. He and Michael engaged in casual conversation, and Michael told him that he was from Tanzania's Ngorongoro Crater area. He showed Bob his identification and since I had my camera out, we took a photograph of him by the lake. Bob stayed until about 10:30 p.m., then I walked him to the gate where his car was parked, and he drove off. I said good night to Michael, who usually resided at the gatehouse, and returned to the house. I was in bed reading when Michael came to the door maybe an hour later.

"MADAM, KIBOKO! KIBOKO!"

There was a hippopotamus in the garden, not an unusual occurrence at the plot. The owner of the property had worked with the *fundi* and local community members to develop an organic garden and small entrepreneurial produce delivery business with all profits going to the gardeners (see figure 7.3). All vegetables and fruit were grown on the property, and then delivered by bicycle in local baskets to (mostly) *wazungu* living in Kisumu. At that time (2007–2009), it was difficult to find nonindigenous vegetables at the local market so they grew arugula, romaine lettuce, and these were combined with local *mito*, *dek*, *osuga*, *ododo*, and *apoth*[3] to be delivered to foreigners—those working for the CDC, the U.S. Army, and a range of nongovernmental organizations delivering services in the Kisumu region. The garden was lush, and the gardeners worked tirelessly at it, trying to keep it weeded, insect free, and watered. The cabbages it seemed were loved by the hippopotamuses and so they would often break through the stone wall, or somehow get over the stone wall, to gorge themselves on the cabbage and in the process destroy the gardens. Thus, when Michael came to the door reporting a *kiboko* had breached the wall, my immediate thought was that the gardens would be destroyed, along with the economic livelihood of the gardeners. On this particular night, the fundi/caretaker who usually stayed on the plot had returned home to his rural village so scaring the *kiboko* back to the lake depended on Michael and myself.

I left the house and we wandered around the property, heading to the area where Michael reported seeing the *kiboko*. But when we arrived, there was nothing. I assumed the hippo had retreated back to the lake and I indicated this to Michael in my broken Kiswahili. I said good night and turned to return to the house. As I did, Michael struck me on the head with his *rungu*. It all happened so fast that I can barely put it all together but what I remember is

Figure 7.3 Organic Produce Home Delivery. *Source*: Provided by Denielle Elliott.

falling to my knees because the blow to my head had been so forceful, losing my glasses, dropping the flashlight and my cell phone, while Michael continued to strike me with his *rungu*. I was shocked and terribly confused. I remember trying to turn so that I could see his face, desperately wanting to understand why he was doing this, needing eye contact. There had been no warning. He didn't seem angry, he didn't seem drunk or high, nor did he seem mentally unstable. Without thinking about it, I started to scream. Michael tried to cover my mouth, and each time he did I bit his hand. This happened three or four or maybe six times. I lost track of time. At one point I remember thinking that I had succeeded in biting down so hard that I had broken his finger. In fact, I think I may have almost bitten his finger off. It is strange to be in a situation like this. Quite honestly, I never thought I had it in me to fight back the way I did. There was never a moment where I thought—I must fight and scream. I just did. And then suddenly, the blows from his *rungu* stopped.

At this point I was bleeding profusely, blood was in my eyes, I had lost my glasses, and it was dark outside (there was no light pollution since no one had electricity in the village) so I couldn't see very well. I didn't know where Michael was but it seemed he had vanished. I managed to pick up my phone and put it back together (the battery had fallen out). I rang my friend Bob who had been with me just an hour or two before, but he didn't answer. I then called the Kenyan lawyer, who lived the closest to me. I told him I had been attacked by Michael and that I needed him to come collect me because I was bleeding badly. He offered to call and ask the neighbors to come and wait with me until he arrived; he also suggested I go back into the house in case Michael was still around. I couldn't get back into the house. The door was locked and I didn't know where the keys were. I yelled for the neighbors in my limited Dholuo, "*Bi! Bi!*" [Come! Come!] And almost immediately my adjacent neighbor, Tobias and three or four other men arrived. I directed the flashlight on to myself so they could see that I was injured. They helped me walk to the gate which was locked (and the key was with Michael). Together they wrenched the large iron gate off the fence, and by the time this was done, my lawyer friend pulled up in his car. We all loaded in and sped to a hospital in town. My friend asked which hospital I should be taken to. I didn't know. I was really trying to process what had just happened. I had heard bad things about all of the hospitals. He decided on the local private hospital, Aga Khan, and he called a colleague at the CDC to meet us there.

My access to care in Kisumu and then in Johannesburg where I was taken for follow up care raises critical questions about my privilege as a white, Canadian born Canadian Institutes of Health Research postdoctoral candidate at the time. I am acutely aware that if a Kenyan had sustained the same injuries, they most likely would have died. If I had not been evacuated to South Africa where I received care from one of the continent's most skilled neurosurgeon, I would have died. Most of my medical expenses, approximately $110,000 USD, was paid for by travel insurance that I purchased in Kisumu for about $70 USD. I did have to pay about $8,000 USD out of pocket, and as a postdoctoral student this was hard for me to do. Thinking about the politics and ethics of medical care in this situation is beyond the scope of this paper but it is equally important in our fieldwork planning.

In the hospital, I was quickly attended to by a team of health professionals. They laid me on a gurney, stabilized my neck and spine with five-kilogram bags of *unga* [flour used for making ugali] on each side of my head: though a private hospital with considerably more resources than the local provincial hospital, they still lacked basic equipment like a cervical collar. The local director for the U.S. Army Research Unit arrived and I remember him carefully washing all the blood off me, telling me they had to figure out where the blood was coming from to see where I was injured. I was beaten badly. My back, my neck, my arm, and of course my skull. The source of blood was a wound on the head. In the end, I was lucky, the only fractures I had were on my skull. These resulted in some additional facial compression fractures.

My time at the hospital is a bit of a blur. I know they wanted to shave the hair off my head to get at the wound and I resisted, begging them not to because I had a job interview for a tenure track position a couple months away at the University of Saskatchewan that I fully intended to attend. I was (mistakenly) confident that I wasn't that hurt. I asked them to just stitch me up and leave the hair. I also remember someone asking me if I wanted to keep the nightgown I had been wearing. It was actually a light-weight dress that I sometimes slept in. I asked them to throw it away. I felt soiled in a deeper way, though at the time I didn't realize it as such. I just wanted them to get rid of the dress/nightgown. I started to vomit, and there was blood coming up that I had swallowed during the attack. Vomiting is a good clinical indicator of more serious head trauma and so I was taken for a CT scan. It was then that the damage to my skull and brain became clearer. I had multiple hematomas that would have to be drained. The next day I was medically evacuated by the Canadian Embassy to Johannesburg after an American neurologist in Kisumu for a study came to assess me (since no Kenyan neurologist was available in western Kenya), and noted that I needed advanced neurological care. I spent a month in the neuro intensive care unit at MilPark Hospital where I received a cranioplasty to rebuild my skull.

I have written elsewhere about hospital care and recovery from brain injury (Elliott 2019). I recovered. I did attend the interview at the University of Saskatchewan. I returned to Kenya and the lakeside house six months later, in October of that same year. I felt I had to for many reasons. In part because I was worried that the longer I waited, the less likely I would have the courage to go back. As a teenager I rode equestrian competitively and so "get back on the horse" was embedded deep in my sense of self. I didn't want to let the fear control me, but I was scared. I was prescribed sleeping pills and a benzodiazepine to help me relax. I needed them; my nerves were raw. And yet I managed with the help of friends, Victor Olago especially, who refused to leave me alone at the lakeside house. He slept in the kitchen each night. I tried to stay there but eventually I had to move to town to a more secure unit. I was reactive, emotional, not quite ready to be back.

The night of the attack, Michael fled on foot. As did my Kenyan lawyer friend's *askari*. They were nowhere to be found. Later people told me how a large group of Kenyan men from the village went to search for Michael. A few years later I caught a ride on a *piki piki* as I was heading out to the house and the driver asked me where I was heading. I told him where I stayed and that I had been staying there off and on for a number of years. And then he asked—"Are you the one?" I asked him to clarify. "The one attacked by the Maasai?" He then went on to tell me how he had participated in the search party that night, and recounted to me how they had searched, where and for how long. It was a strange moment for me. I had not heard the story before. And I could sense from this motorbike rider that he felt he knew me, that we shared a history, that we were tied together by a deeply intimate event.

Michael was never found. I was asked if I wanted the Kisumu police to continue pursuing the case and if I would be willing to return to testify against

him in court should he be found. I wasn't. I didn't feel vengeful. I was trying to make sense of what happened in my own way. As an anthropologist
the attack was caught up in academic conversations about poverty, gender
norms, race, the injustices of criminal systems, blame/guilt, and colonial histories of anthropology. I feared the story would be a story about a black man
attacking a white woman so when the Canadian Broadcasting Corporation
news reached out to my postdoctoral supervisor at UBC to ask for information about what had happened, I asked him not to share anything. Micaela
di Leonardo has written provocatively about her experience being raped and
how she managed others' assumptions about race/sex amid racial divisions
and injustices in the United States (di Leonardo 1997). Around the same time
that I was hurt, a woman was attacked and killed in the Pacific Spirit Park,
adjacent to the University of British Columbia campus, a place I frequently
went running and still walk my dog when I am back in Vancouver.[4] So when
people asked me about what happened, I explained that it could happen anywhere, that it *does* happen everywhere. I worked hard to counter any narrative
that suggested Kenya was somehow more dangerous than Canada.

But as much as I did not want it to be about race, ideas of race did shape
the way I made sense of the encounter (also see Johnson 2016; di Leonardo
1997). A colleague once said something to me that I thought was very
insightful and provocative. We were talking about violent experiences with
men and she asked me if I would have felt different about the incident (specifically pursing justice through the courts) had the attacker been white. I
imagined then how I would have felt had it been one of my white Canadian
or American colleagues in Kenya and without hesitation I realized I would
have demanded that he be pursued and punished. Ideas of race may have also
shaped Michael's understanding of what he was doing and why he did it. He
saw a white, educated, wealthy, foreign woman—a *mzungu*.[5] Diane Nelson
(1999), writing about her research in Guatemala, speaks directly about the
"*gringa*" in the field and the complex power relations that run through such
gendered, othered categories, as a politically powerful American who can
travel where many Guatemalans cannot, and yet her feelings of vulnerability in the field. She argues that the gringa identity is "neither innocent nor
transcendent," that it is "complicitous and inescapable" (1999: 48), and it is
wrapped up in geopolitical politics between the United States and Central
America. Though we might act in "solidarity," as part of our commitment to
engaged or committed anthropology (49), our presence and acts, like choosing places to live in the field, are non-innocent.

This chapter is not meant to be a story about dangerous fieldwork, or
fieldwork about violence.[6] I instead understand my experience as a story
about being a woman in a world where we often find ourselves at risk of
violence. I have experienced verbal, physical, and sexual assaults, abuses,

and innuendos from men, almost all of them unconnected to fieldwork, and almost all of them by white men (also see di Leonardo 2018). It was awful what happened that night, but I have had worse experiences, as many women worldwide have. What made this experience different for me is that I understood the violent encounter *through anthropology*. I couldn't help but think about Michelle Rosaldo's accidental death in 1981 and the power of Renato Rosaldo's reflections on grief and anger (1989). From my disciplinary training, I took away two lessons.

First was that I was in a sense culpable. I had made the decision to carry out fieldwork in a place with intense inequalities, inequalities that aligned with race, nation, and capitalist extraction. I continued to be engaged in a disciplinary practice that still in complicated ways was enmeshed with settler-colonial projects and imperialism (Asad 1973). Second, the field of anthropology deepened my capacity for empathy. I have always been an empathic person, even as a child, but anthropology nourished and finely tuned my empathy. From anthropology I learned to think about powerful forces that shape our lives, histories, political-economies, and extractive capitalisms. Kenya was a British colony and under that rule Kenyans experienced terror and violence (Elkins 2005; Anderson 2012). Though independent since 1963, one still sensed how colonial history shaped everyday encounters between white Kenyans, black Kenyans, and foreigners like me working or studying there. As illustration, take my experiences at a post-office. In Kisumu there always seemed to be a lineup at the post-office and I frequently had to ship materials to London, UK during my first year in Kenya. I would, like everyone else, get in the queue. On some days, Kenyans would insist I go before them, deferring to me as if I was someone important and not just a foreign postdoc, and this made me incredibly uncomfortable. But then on other days, Kenyans would enter, look at me disapprovingly, and then cut in front of me in the line. I understood both reactions to me, an educated, white foreigner, perceived as a remnant of former British colonial agents. Added to the history of colonialism's racist practices and policies was the fact that the average Kenyan lived below the poverty line. In Kisumu the large majority live in sprawling informal settlements with no running water, often no power, engaged in the informal economy known as the *jua kali* [loosely translated as working under the hot sun]. So when Michael attacked me, I felt like I couldn't really blame him. I recognize my ability to forgive him is not just a matter of disciplinary training but about me, as a particular type of person. Others may have the same training in anthropology as me and feel unable to forgive their attackers. I understand that too. Michael feels like such a minor actor in this story. I realize that may be hard for many readers to understand, but I understood his violence toward me as a response to the history of terror of colonialism and to the extreme inequities of global capitalism, where North American and European companies continue to accrue enormous capital gains through resource extraction (either environmental or through scientific research); while acknowledging Michael had agency and that there are millions of people in the world who also experienced colonialism and the inequities of a particularly brutal capitalism and yet are never violent.

It was a significant and life-changing experience for me. My experience speaks to an important dilemma for many researchers conducting fieldwork in places not their own, but especially for women (though not exclusively of course for women, see Baird 2018). I share the story, somewhat hesitantly, not because it offers answers but because I hope it raises questions for others as they plan fieldwork (especially for those planning it for the first time). We must think critically about how gendered the fieldsite is and what it means for us to ethically negotiate our fieldwork sites in ways that are honest, safe, and attuned to local and global histories that we are a part of (Clark and Grant 2015). I think it is important for us to think about the relationship between the seemingly mundane decisions of fieldwork like where to live with the empirical questions we are asking about power, representation, identity, and political-economic inequalities in the twenty-first century. As educators and graduate supervisors, we also need to speak frankly to our students about the safety and living arrangements, as much as we do about theory and method. It is important for us to remember that the field is messy and complicated and sometimes, no matter how carefully we try to navigate the challenges and tensions, we find ourselves unable to escape it.

NOTES

1. Almost everything I write materializes from conversations I have, usually real, sometimes imaginary, with colleagues and friends also thinking about ethnographic fieldwork. When I was first hurt, many people suggested that, as an anthropologist, I write about what had happened. It has taken me ten years to be ready to write about these experiences and I'm still reticent, worried about how the story will be received. I am grateful to many colleagues who have shaped my approach to fieldwork, to ethics, and assisted me in Kenya, especially Victor Olago, Patrick Mbullo Owuor, Philister Adhiambo, and Dara Culhane. Jordan Hodgins, Victor Olago and Lindsay Bell graciously took time to offer suggestions and edits on earlier drafts of this paper. All remaining errors and weaknesses are mine.

2. I have written about these trials elsewhere. See Elliott 2014a and 2014b.

3. These are the Dholuo terms. In Kiwswahili and English these are *sukuma wiki* (African kale), *boo* (cowpeas), *mito* (slenderleaf), *dek* (spiderplant), *osuga* (African nightshades), *ododo* (amaranths), and *apoth* (Jute Mallow).

4. In April 2009, Wendy Ladner-Beaudry was killed. Her attacker has never been found.

5. Diane Nelson's exploration of *gringa* begs a similar unpacking of *mzungu/wazungu* in Kenya, especially in more rural and remote settings, including western Kenya where being called mzungu by Kenyans, adults and children, happens multiple times per day. For white anthropologists working in Kenya, this categorization shapes fieldwork and undoubtedly our relations with interlocutors though I have rarely, if ever, read anthropologists write about how so.

6. Jeffrey Sluka writes about the dangers encountered by anthropologists interested in state violence (2015) which is quite a different context than what I was working in. In 2009, the post-election violence in Kenya was over. Tourism had rebounded and I did not feel like Kenya was a dangerous place to be. Sluka also makes recommendations in this paper on how to manage and prepare one's self for dangerous fieldwork settings.

BIBLIOGRAPHY

Anderson, David. 2012. "British Abuse and Torture in Kenya's Counter-Insurgency, 1952–1960." *Small Wars & Insurgencies*, 23(4–5): 700–719.

Armbruster, Heidi and Anna Lærke, eds. 2010. *Taking Sides: Ethics, Politics, and Fieldwork in Anthropology*. New York, NY: Berghahn Books.

Asad, Talal, ed. 1973. *Anthropology and the Colonial Encounter*. London: Ithaca Press.

Baird, A., 2018. Dancing with danger: ethnographic safety, male bravado and gang research in Colombia. *Qualitative Research*, 18(3), pp.342–360.

Briggs, Jean. 1971. *Never in Anger: Portrait of an Eskimo Family*. Cambridge, MA: Harvard University Press.

Cerwonka, A. and Malkki, L.H., 2008. *Improvising theory: Process and temporality in ethnographic fieldwork*. University of Chicago Press.

Chagnon, Napolean. 1997. *Yanomamö* (Case Studies in Cultural Anthropology). San Diego, CA: Harcourt Brace.

Clark, Imogen and Andrea Grant. 2015. "Sexuality and Danger in the Field: Starting an Uncomfortable Conversation." *Journal of the Anthropological Society of Oxford*, 7(1): 1–14.

Clifford, James. 1983. "On Ethnographic Authority." *Representations*, 2: 118–146.

Culhane, Dara. 2017. "Imagining: An Introduction." In *A Different Kind of Ethnography: Imaginative Practices and Creative Methodologies*, edited by Denielle Elliott and Dara Culhane. Toronto: University of Toronto Press.

di Leonardo, Micaela. 2018. "#MeToo is Nowhere Near Enough." *HAU: Journal of Ethnographic Theory*, 8(3): 420–425.

di Leonardo, Micaela. 1997. "White Lies, Black Myths: Rape, Race and the Black 'Underclass'." In *The Gender/Sexuality Reader: Culture, History and Political-Economy*, edited by Roger Lancaster and Micaela di Leonardo. New York, NY: Routledge Press.

Elkins, Caroline. 2005. *Britain's Gulag: The Brutal End of Empire in Kenya*. London: Random House.

Elliott, Denielle. 2019. "Neurological Disturbances and Time Travel." *Catalyst: Feminist, Theory, Technoscience*, 5(2): 1–27.

Elliott, Denielle. 2014a. "The Protected Lab: Securitization and Spaces of Exclusion in Global Medicine." *Medical Anthropology Theory*, 1(1): 81–113.

Elliott, Denielle. 2014b. "Imagining 'Atlanta': The Politics and Poetics of Experimental Medicine in East Africa." *Cultural Studies Review*, 20(1): 277–301.

Fabian, Johannes. 1983. *Time and the Other: How Anthropology Makes its Object*. New York, NY: Columbia University Press.

Fabian, Johannes. 2007. *Memory against Culture: Arguments and Reminders*. Durham, NC: Duke University Press.

Fortun, Kim. 2003. "Ethnography In/Of/As Open Systems." *Reviews in Anthropology*, 32: 171–190.

Ghassem-Fachandi, Parvis, ed. 2009. *Violence: Ethnographic Encounters*. Oxford: Berg Publishers.

Gupta, Akhil and James Ferguson. 1997. "Discipline and Practice: 'The Field' As Site, Method, and Location in Anthropology." In *Anthropological Locations: Boundaries and Grounds of a Field Science*, edited by Akhil Gupta and James Ferguson, 1–46. Berkeley, CA: University of California.

Heath, Deborah. 1998. "Locating Genetic Knowledge: Picturing Marfan Syndrome and Its Traveling Constituencies." *Science, Technology, & Human Values*, 23(1): 71–97.

Johnson, Alix. 2016. "The Self at Stake: Thinking Fieldwork and Sexual Violence." *Savage Minds*, March 16. Accessed July 12, 2020. https://savageminds.org/2016/0 3/16/the-self-at-stake-thinking-fieldwork-and-sexual-violence/.

Koonings, Kees, Dirk Kruijt, and Dennis Rodgers. 2019. *Ethnography as Risky Business: Field Research in Violent and Sensitive Contexts*. New York, NY: Lexington Books.

Kovats-Bernat, J. Christopher. 2002. "Negotiating Dangerous Fields: Pragmatic Strategies for Fieldwork amid Violence and Terror." *American Anthropologist*, 104(1): 208–222.

Kulick, D. and M. Wilson, eds. 1995. *Taboo: Sex, Identity, and Erotic Subjectivity in Fieldwork*. London: Routledge.

Lee, Raymond. 1994. *Dangerous Fieldwork*. Thousand Oaks, CA: Sage.

Mahmood, C. K. 2008. "Anthropology from the Bones: A Memoir of Fieldwork, Survival, and Commitment." *Anthropology and Humanism*, 33(1–2): 1–11.

Marshall, Mac. 1993. "The Wizard from Oz Meets the Wicked Witch of the East: Freeman, Mead, and Ethnographic Authority." *American Ethnologist*, 20(3): 604–615.

Morena, Eva. 1995. "Rape in the Field: Reflections from a Survivor." In *Taboo: Sex, Identity, and Erotic Subjectivity in Anthropological Fieldwork*, edited by Don Kulick and Margaret Wilson. New York, NY: Routledge.

Munene, George. 2020. "Re-Emergence of Brutal Mungiki Gang Strikes Fear into Traders and Residents." *Daily Nation*, June 3, 2020. Accessed July 12, 2020. https ://www.nation.co.ke/kenya/news/re-emergence-of-brutal-mungiki-gang-strikes-fear-into-traders-and-residents-491268.

Munishi, E. J. 2016. "Coping with Urban Crime and Resilience Factors: The Case of the Maasai Security Guards in Dar es Salaam, Tanzania." *Journal of Sociology and Development*, 1(1): 60–79.

Nelson, Diane. 1999. "Gringa Positioning, Vulnerable Bodies, and Fluidarity: A Partial Relation." In *A Finger in the Wound: Body Politics in Quincentennial Guatemala*. Berkeley, CA: University of California Press.

Nordstrom, Carolyn and Antonius Robben. 1995. *Fieldwork under Fire: Contemporary Studies of Violence and Survival*. Berkeley, CA: University of California Press.

Rosaldo, Renato. 1989. "Introduction: Grief and a Headhunter's Rage." In *Culture and Truth: The Remaking of Social Analysis*. Boston, MA: Beacon Press.

Sluka, Jeffrey. 2015. "Managing Danger in Fieldwork with Perpetrators of Political Violence and State Terror." *Conflict and Society*, 1(1): 109–124.

Sultan, Aisha. 2019. "When Fieldwork Breaks Your Heart." *Cultural Anthropology Podcast*. https://culanth.org/fieldsights/when-fieldwork-breaks-your-heart.

Conclusion

Finding Truths in Different Forms

Ida Fadzillah Leggett

INTRODUCTION

When first entering the field, one believes in the process of discovering truths, of uncovering the infallible logics that govern everyday life. The novice anthropologist is prepared for that, for truths are often perceived as universal and thus familiar. But once the months pass and the fieldworker is blended into the native scenery, indigenous realities reveal themselves in all their complex messiness. These moments when the veil is raised often require a more creative and personal retelling rather than one of academic exposition. This is partly because unexpected revelations require more reflective or affective language to capture their significance: we do not simply witness these moments; rather we feel the weight of them as important. Another reason we fall back on more intimate language is because oftentimes these recollections reveal our own personal and vulnerable truths, and sometimes the only words that will do are those that are sparse, emotional, and unsparing.

These fieldwork stories are part and parcel of the anthropological experience I have come to value. Malaysian by birth, I lived most of my childhood abroad following my diplomatic family on postings to Ottawa, Tripoli, and Seoul. In this drifting life, Malaysian newspaper stories, gossip, and stereotypes came to frame my understanding of my homeland. My parents themselves rarely spoke of their lives growing up in the state of Kedah, choosing to look forward rather than back onto their childhoods growing up in the *kampong* (village). I first encountered anthropology in high school in New York City. My family had just moved to the United States a couple of years earlier, and I was a quiet, awkward, and isolated student unsure about the social norms of this new place. The rules I was used to did not fit American life, and I felt adrift and invisible. When I began my cultural anthropology course my junior year, however, I was introduced to a way of viewing the world that included anyone and everyone as equally worthy of inspection. I still have my dog-eared ethnographies from those years—of the Yanomamo and the Bunyaro—with blue ink marring each page with squiggly underlines and question marks. I did not understand the world I was in, but I felt empowered by learning about other places that at first seemed so insignificant and yet turned out to be so revealing about humanity. In short, I was hooked. In college, I picked up James Scott's (1985) "Weapons of the Weak," highlighting his field research in "Sedaka," a pseudonymous *kampong* in Kedah, and my world came full circle. The detail in Scott's description of the life of real people sitting around and interacting opened my eyes to the possibility of a new framework for understanding (my) human experience. Scott made clear that "even" non-Western peoples have stories and experiences that are complex and interesting, and as important to our understanding of the human experience as graphs, statistics, or surveys. And I so appreciated meeting others who saw the beauty in the obscure and insignificant; this was the community I wanted to be part of.

Three decades later, I understand that these studies were flawed and incomplete—my high school and college classes never touched on the history of anthropology and colonialism, imperialism, and racist policies. We never read about the problematics of the exotic or the essentialized, and so the smooth face of cultural anthropology remained preserved as "truth" and "science." It was not until my graduate school days at the University of Illinois at Urbana-Champaign that anthropology was revealed as historical and political, and for me became even more interesting.

In the twenty-first century the form anthropology takes has changed again, partly in the expression of our data, analysis, and conclusions. It is my belief that we must expand the ways in which we talk about anthropological things. This volume has been one attempt at such an endeavor in that its mission is to reach out to a broader audience to tell the story and the significance of the story. The volume also experiments with different voices and styles to capture cultural truths (this time in the plural) that might be harder to explain with more academic jargon. And finally, it prioritizes nontraditional anthropological subjects like friendship and travel, secrets and intimate moments, frustrations and inconclusive situations. In these stories of everyday moments and ever-changing situations, I hope the importance of understanding cultures and what it teaches us about being human comes across. Ethnographers provide vivid and often unexpected detail of other societies that others might write off as simple or backward, for "anthropologists are distinguished by their readiness to learn from those who, in a world fixated on the advance of knowledge, might otherwise be dismissed as uneducated, illiterate or even ignorant" (Ingold 2018: 10). The detail, the color, the focus on communities that other disciplines might see as irrelevant, the recording of voices usually ignored, these are all things that anthropology does even when it is not easy or necessarily welcomed by academia.

But we are more than fieldworkers: we are also tasked with teaching the next generation about anthropology. Here our strength as teachers does not only lie in the details we seek to impart; it also lies in our methodology: we do fieldwork to collect our data, and we tell field stories in our classrooms to communicate our conclusions. And I would argue that this latter method should be explored further, for the fieldwork tale is a powerful teaching tool. As Foster (2019) muses, "Stories multiply, are myriad and interminable; the stories we tell and those we listen to set us up for whatever agency we can achieve" (248). Anthropology connects the global to the local of our students. And as teachers of anthropology to the next generation, I believe our strengths lay in our ability show our students the world through this lens, and as closely to the perspectives of the "natives" themselves. This perspective also means that I see our job—of teaching about other societies and their (and our) myriad rules of behavior—to include teaching about the ephemeral and the unexplainable. This perspective is also about showing the significance of the everyday, prioritizing this at the same level as the sacred and the memorialized. I would argue that to truly understand what is going on, we must open the eyes of our students to the beauty of daily routine, as well as unexpected moments. This is how we transmit the discipline to the next generation of anthropologists, understanding that "lest we think that theory exchange is only happening in the pages of academic journals and monographs, I would argue that every lecture by a professor to students is also the site of the exchange of theory" (Falcone 2013: 126).

This volume also emphasizes creativity and experimentality, the editors acknowledgement that telling good stories sometimes requires unconventional approaches. This is something we do consistently in the classroom but tend to shy away from in our writing. This is a mistake, for I believe our strength and uniqueness is in our ability to perceive the unexpected as well as explaining the previously unexplainable. Therefore the focus in this volume on "the stories we teach" is meant to add to popular understanding of what anthropologists do—through the perspective of the teaching to the next generation of students—and thus to demonstrate why anthropology is important, and interesting, and relevant now more than ever.

THE FRAME AND FOCUS OF ANTHROPOLOGY

There are several reasons that the discipline of anthropology resonates with so much of what is happening in the world today. Anthropologists ask new and unexpected questions and thus bring to light often-missed information about the culture and people under study. By doing this, we often clarify the gray areas of life and better understand the important details embedded in the everyday. This ability is a skill and a strength that make anthropologists integral to accurately understanding the world. Without this perspective, people have a tendency to imagine the world as a series of vignettes or snapshots of an essentialized "Other" that can be understood through generalizations, akin to relating these cultures directly to postcards of the Great Wall or the Eiffel Tower. What is clear to me is that the ethnographer is trained to understand the artificiality of this "postcard" perspective. One way is through our recognition of the importance of seeing from within the society. Simply put, anthropological training asserts that to really know what is going on in a society, you have to go to that society, and you have to stay for a long time. Our frame does not allow us to stand on the outside looking in. An interesting advantage of this perspective is that anthropologists can inject the significance of time into their frame, acknowledging that in any place, the scenery is constantly shifting, people grow old, minds change, and ideas get discarded. Additionally, I believe our key contribution, the meat of our trade, is the anthropologist's ability to focus in on the details. And not just the details, the details of the details: we find further truths within frames that others take for granted as bedrock. My students train to fully see what is in front of them, and to record what they see; but many do not understand that their intricate observations are data gold. That level of observation is what is missing from postcard perspectives, for if one is within the frame, one's focus can work inward into the community in a way that captures the realities of power structures at the level of the lived experience.

To question one's own frame of reference on the world is to acknowledge that various factors come into play that influence and craft one's perspective, questions, and conclusions. However, this is our skill: developing the ethnographic perspective allows the researcher to understand a culture beyond its postcard symbolism. As Stoller puts it, the work of anthropology has created an "enviable record of scholarship" (2018: xviii). While difficult, the anthropologist learns to adjust her frame and focus outward as well as inward and move with the society's flows of time and people's movements across space and place, and refocus on the areas of significance that the people themselves know to be important. She dives into that spot and unpacks even more detail, to completely reframe the moment.

The format of storytelling is not divorced from the field experience; indeed, the situations that anthropologists often encounter in the field—as well as in everyday life—play out like a good story. Rautman (2008) muses that "there are events in our lives that can take on the proportions of an epic tale, a saga, existing in mythic time and space . . ." and as anthropologists "we sort out the jumble of events into a narrative framework, with commentary, highlighting first one aspect, then another"(85). This "sorting out of events" is necessary not only to tell a good story, but to tell an accurate one. This volume's emphasis on exploring new ways to express the discoveries of the field is not new—others have experimented over the last decade with how to "write anthropology" (see, for example, McGranahan 2020; Pandian 2019; Starn 2015; Waterston and Vesperi 2009; Wulff 2016). But these chapters pay equal attention to how we "narrate anthropology," and thus the language used here takes on the tone and the cadence of a good tale.

This exploration of different ways of telling is increasingly important today. We are "strange travelers" (Syring 2018) which is a good thing because being a "strange traveler is an advantage, allowing us the anthropological perspective we treasure" (176). However, our strengths tend to be "weirdly submerged in much of the writing we do, obscured by our academic arguments" (176). Our academic writings are often verbose and convoluted; and this leads us to ask the important question: "Is anyone out there reading our stuff? (Stoller 2018: xiv). For Paul Stoller, the answer is "no": "Here's the issue: most scholars, including, of course, most anthropologists, do not write clear and compelling prose. Perhaps the greatest key to developing a truly public anthropology lies less in adopting increasingly sophisticated digital platforms than in training scholars to write for broader audiences" (Stoller 2018: 192). To counter this negative trend, Stoller advocates for more stories: "Bad writing disconnects readers from writers. No matter the format, works that remain open to the world are usually those in which writers use narratives—stories—to connect with their readers. Those are the texts that endure . . ." (2018: xvii). Others also believe in the wisdom of expressing ethnographic moments creatively. Beatty states: "The novelist and the ethnographer find common cause in a special concern with particulars, the odds and ends that get left behind in theoretical discussion as excess baggage" (2019: 116).

This approach also means that we should explore different ways of telling our truths—and thus the focus in this volume on narrating field stories in the classroom. Anthropology is important in its holistic amalgamation of sight, sound, time, and space, and there are a lot of anthropologists trying to capture new aspects of anthropology these days through more artistic and experimental ways of capturing cultural details (see, for example, Berlant and Stewart 2019; Elliott and Culhane 2016; Klima 2019; McLean 2017; Pandian 2019; Stoller 2018). Stoller (2018) advocates for reaching a wider audience through blogging and other forms of media including "narrative ethnography, fiction, ethnographic film/video, performance, poetry, and multimedia art installations" (185). To this list, I would include mediums like podcasts, Twitter, tumblr, magazines, YouTube or even Tik Tok. This expansion of the expression of anthropology also means that we should not shy away from our own personal events in the field that hover ghostlike in our memories, or ignore the warnings of our dreams, or forget the moments that make us tumble to our knees. The authors in this volume are focusing on how these unconventional mediums are themselves a powerful teaching tool for our students, and therefore should be seen as central to the anthropological project in general. Because to be a contributing voice of the twenty-first century, we need to adapt and adjust our words to be included more, because the world needs us and our truths and our ethics. To become part of the global conversation, we need to write and speak more simply and more clearly, in the language of community in addition to the academic writing and lecturing that we currently do.

I agree with Ruth Behar, who writes: "When you write vulnerably, others respond vulnerably" (1996: 16). I would add that when we speak vulnerably and share tales that evoke emotion, our audience opens their hearts and their ears to our lessons. Through our classroom stories, we teach our students that: the world of human beings is bigger than their town or their state. And by human beings we mean people who are as human (loving, kind, stupid, confused) as they are, not plastic stereotypes they see on television or social media. Our students are part of this larger, diverse, interesting, confusing, wonder-filled world, and understanding who they are and their humanity starts only after they realize their own culturally created internal logics (that what they assumed was universally true is actually only culturally true). Your own cultural logics extend everywhere and into everything, as they do for other cultures as well. We examine how effective communication across cultures as well as across diverse social groups can only happen with an understanding of the previous points. And finally, we confront the reality that to be a real global citizen requires the acceptance of these hard truths and the opening of this sense of wonder about the world. True engagement with the anthropological material means that your students acquire an expansive and flexible perspective on the material; that is, they then learn how to "play" with the theories themselves, and apply our lessons to other facets of their lives or lessons. And that sense of enchantment is what makes them try this in the first place. When we do it right, we transform the mundane into the wondrous.

ENCHANTMENT AND WONDER

It is important to acknowledge that anthropologists can write and narrate clearly and beautifully; and further, that I believe anthropologists should write and narrate clearly and beautifully. More humanistically-inclined anthropologists like Edith Turner have known this for a while, advocating for a discipline that communicates the life-breath of culture as well as its nuts and bolts: "The purpose of anthropology is to supply humankind with information about itself. However, *humanistic* anthropology draws nearer to the living human being. It seeks to give humankind an understanding of the heart of the human being in relation to his or her fellows" (2007: 108). For Turner, this is a valuable perspective that allows an audience to more readily "get the hang of" another culture (108). Ingold (2018), for whom anthropology is "philosophy with the people in" (4) brings the humanistic aspect to the field, arguing that anthropologists should "share" in the presence of another culture, "to learn from their experiments in living, and to bring this experience to bear on our own imaginings of what human life could be like, its future conditions and possibilities" (2018: 8). And Ruth Behar, in her profoundly moving text *The Vulnerable Observer: Anthropology that Breaks Your Heart* (1996) interprets anthropology as "the most fascinating, bizarre, disturbing, and necessary form of witnessing left to us at the end of the twentieth century" (3). For her, doing anthropology is like a voyage where

"Loss, mourning, the longing for memory, the desire to enter the world around you and having no idea how to do it, the fear of observing too coldly or too distractedly or too raggedly, the rage of cowardice, the insight that is always arriving late, as defiant hindsight, a sense of the utter uselessness of writing anything and yet the burning desire to write something, are the stopping places along the way. At the end of the voyage, if you are lucky, you catch a glimpse of a lighthouse, and you are grateful" (Behar 1996: 3).

What these interpretations of anthropology share is a recognition of the significance—in addition to the hard data mined from fieldwork—of the intertwined experiences of the fieldworker and the community that lead to a more thorough understanding of that culture. Field stories can demonstrate, as they further intertwine the audience with the anthropologist and the narrative, that moments of day-dreaming, of confusing encounters, of conversations about the future can tell us a lot about that culture and also about ourselves. One thing this volume is trying to do is to suss out ways to honestly understand the truth of everyday life, even those facets from which we want to avert our eyes. And the best way to understand these engagements is through giving in to the significance of enchantment (Stainova 2019) and wonder (Biehl and Locke 2017: 7) found in the unexpected moments in the field. This is possible because fieldwork "moves us away from the entrenched categories and expands the perspectives—on other cultures, space-times, and species—from which we can perceive and understand the world (if only always partially)" (Biehl and Locke 2017: 6–7). Yana Stainova explores an encounter she had in the field, when sharing daydreams with her Venezuelan interlocutors that she found mutually soothing and ethnographically revelatory: "In that backyard on the edges of a small Venezuelan town, we had conjured a force in the world that allowed us to imagine things otherwise. It transformed us, made us accomplices in what we had created. It was an act of mutual enchantment that transcended, for a moment, the structural limitations of our dreams" (216). She shared with her fieldwork community in the verbal imagining of a desirable future, and mused that "this encounter required of me to momentarily suspend disbelief and to allow myself to play with my interlocutors, to let the conversation go in unpredictable directions, to riff off the jokes they made" (217). She elaborated, "It asked me . . . to participate instead in worlds of fantasy and the imagination that purposefully broke with the structures of everyday life" (217). The world of dreams is a world of possible futures, and a view of an "anthropology of becoming" in which Biehl and Locke urge ethnographers to make use of the "ethnographic sensorium," that "multifaceted and affective point of contact with worlds of inequality, hovering on the verge of exhaustion while also harboring the potential for things to be otherwise" (2017: 3). However, affect is not always positive, it can also be stress-laden like the experience of "precarity." As Stewart (2015) explains it, "I take precarity to be one register of the singularity of emergent phenomena—their plurality, movement, imperfection, immanence, incommensurateness, the way they accrete, accrue, and wear out" (Stewart 2015: 221). Additionally, "Precarity can take the form of a sea change, a darkening atmosphere, a hard fall, or the barely perceptible sense of a reprieve. Attachments, or ways of living, can be precious without melodrama, ordinary things that matter because they shimmer precariously. Precarity, written as an emergent form, can raise the question of how to approach ordinary tactile composition, everyday worldlings that matter in many ways beyond their status as representations or objects of moralizing" (Stewart 2015: 222).

So the anthropology of becoming is one that emphasizes movement and change, interruptions and revelations that can be found in all cultures. It can also apply to the uninitiated—students in our classes can be understood through an anthropology of becoming. We can see it in their eyes and the movement of their bodies if they "get it." For one short moment they experience what we experienced in the field: "To pay attention to things—to watch for their movements and listen to their sounds—is to catch the world in the act, like riding the cusp of a wave ever on the point of breaking. Far from coming late upon a world wherein the die is already cast, it is to be there, present and alert, at the very moment of its taking shape. In that moment experience and imagination fuse, and the world comes to life" (Ingold 2018: 22). And what they "get" a lot of times is through this a sense of wonder (that was transformed from its previous state of disgust, or confusion, or ridicule ("that's weird"). Through our students' experiences connecting with a good story I emphasize this concept in anthropology of "becoming," and it is through the transformation of our students' perspective—from confusion to wonder—that I believe our anthropology finally "sinks in." Other anthropologists have attempted to go the route of a more "intimate ethnography" (Waterston and Rylko-Bauer 2006), and to use the imagination, and wonder, and enchantment, to reach a point, of "ethnographic sincerity" (Jackson Jr. 2010) or, as Patico (2018) writes, of "a politics of critical empathy that ideally lends itself to opening up new conversations among distinct, mutually skeptical audiences" (75). All of which leads up to a call for more vulnerability.

What does ethnographic vulnerability entail? For Ruth Behar, "Vulnerability doesn't mean that anything personal goes. The exposure of the self who is also a spectator has to take us somewhere we couldn't otherwise get to. It has to be essential to the argument, not a decorative flourish, not exposure for its own sake" (Behar 1996: 14). In her research on American men who used online agencies to seek wives from the former Soviet Union, Patico (2018) argues that "a key goal of feminist anthropology should be to use ethnography to create humanizing portrayals of those whom our audiences might otherwise find confusing or offensive—even as we keep dynamics of power and inequity in view. This is a politics of critical empathy that ideally lends itself to opening up new conversations among distinct, mutually skeptical audiences" (75). I would argue that because of this strategic vulnerability, we make a connection with our very human students, and we communicate our lessons better. Our narratives are a more accessible kind of writing and teaching that helps to minimize the boundaries between researcher and researched, and between the storyteller and his audience. And this is important because in this moment, it is crucial that we combat outdated biases and old designations and enter into the twenty-first century: where cities are culturally diverse and even the smallest villages are daily influenced by global forces.

CONCLUSION: THE POWER OF THE STORY

The best anthropology transforms the Other into "one of us," and invites everyone into the conversation. With twenty-first century anthropology I agree with Starn that the future of the discipline is unpredictable because anthropology "sometimes feels like a wacky grab bag of diverging concerns and agendas in the first place" (2015: 19). While others have tried to predict and describe our present discipline (see, for example, Fischer 2018; Hannerz 2010; Lewin and Silverstein 2016; Pandian 2019; Pertierra 2018), we really have no idea. All we can do is try and shape the discipline to reach as many diverse people as possible. So, to bring this back to the beginning, one way to do this is to allow language into our communications that makes room for the humanizing side of the field: the stories, the emotions, the wonder, and the uncertain. I do not necessarily call for a prioritizing of such affective aspects of culture;

rather I would like to bring it out in the open. And I know this is hard because focusing on the stories that tie us together also forces us—the researchers and thus experts—to recognize our own humanity and vulnerability in the field and in our own writing. But the world has changed, "natives" are also anthropologists, and our own backyard cries out for ethnographic attention. Recognizing the power in the vulnerable voice situated in our field stories invites diverse new people into our fold, and expands the community of anthropologists in a way that will hopefully bring relevance to our field for decades to come.

REFERENCES

Beatty, Andrew. 2019. *Emotional Worlds: Beyond an Anthropology of Emotion.* Cambridge: Cambridge University Press.

Behar, Ruth. 1996. *The Vulnerable Observer: Anthropology that Breaks Your Heart.* Boston, MA: Beacon Press.

Berlant, Lauren and Kathleen Stewart. 2019. *The Hundreds.* Durham, NC: Duke University Press.

Biehl, Joao and Peter Locke. 2017. "Introduction: Ethnographic Sensorium." In *Unfinished: The Anthropology of Becoming*, edited by Joao Biehl and Peter Locke. Durham, NC: Duke University Press.

Elliott, Denielle and Dara Culhane, eds. 2016. *A Different Kind of Ethnography: Imaginative Practices and Creative Methodologies.* Toronto: University of Toronto Press.

Falcone, Jessica Marie. 2013. "The Hau of Theory: The Kept-Gift of Theory Itself in American Anthropology." *Anthropology and Humanism*, 38(2): 122–145.

Fischer, Michael M. J. 2018. *Anthropology in the Meantime: Experimental Ethnography, Theory, and Method for the Twenty-First Century.* Durham, NC: Duke University Press.

Foster, Stephen William. 2019. "On Listening: Polyphony and the Vagaries of Representation." *Anthropology and Humanism*, 44(2): 248–259.

Hannerz, Ulf. 2010. *Anthropology's World: Life in a Twenty-First Century Discipline.* London: Pluto Press.

Ingold, Tim. 2018. *Anthropology: Why it Matters.* Cambridge, UK: Polity Press.

Jackson Jr., John L. 2010. "On Ethnographic Sincerity." *Current Anthropology*, 51(2): 279–287.

Klima, Alan. 2019. *Ethnography #9.* Durham, NC: Duke University Press.

Lewin, Ellen and Leni M. Silverstein, eds. 2016. *Mapping Feminist Anthropology in the Twenty-first Century.* New Brunswick, NJ: Rutgers University Press.

McGranahan, Carole, ed. 2020. *Writing Anthropology: Essays on Craft and Commitment.* Durham, NC: Duke University Press.

McLean, Stuart. 2017. *Fictionalizing Anthropology: Encounters and Fabulations on the Edges of the Human.* Minneapolis, MN: University of Minnesota Press.

Pandian, Anand. 2019. *A Possible Anthropology: Methods for Uneasy Times.* Durham, NC: Duke University Press.

Patico, Jennifer. 2018. "Awkward Sincerity and Critical Empathy: Encounters in 'International Marriage Brokering' and Feminist Anthropology." *Critique of Anthropology*, 38(1): 75–95.

Pertierra, Anna Cristina. 2018. *Media Anthropology for the Digital Age.* New York, NY: Wiley Publishing.

Rautman, Alison E. 2008. "Thick Description of a Visit Home: In Tribute to Clifford Geertz." *Anthropology and Humanism*, 33(1): 85–94.

Scott, James. 1985. *Weapons of the Weak: Everyday Forms of Peasant Resistance.* New Haven, CT: Yale University Press.

Stainova, Yana. 2019. "Enchantment as Method." *Anthropology and Humanism*, 44(2): 214–230.

Starn, Orin. 2015. "Introduction." In *Writing Culture and the Life of Anthropology*, edited by Orin Starn, 1–24. Durham, NC: Duke University Press.

Stewart, Kathleen. 2015. *Ordinary Affects.* Durham, NC: Duke University Press.

Stoller, Paul. 2018. *Adventures in Blogging: Public Anthropology and Popular Media.* Toronto: University of Toronto Press.

Syring, David. 2018. "Anthropologists as Strange Travelers." *Anthropology and Humanism*, 43(2): 176–177.

Turner, Edith. 2007. "Introduction to the Art of Ethnography." *Anthropology and Humanism*, 32(2): 108–116.

Waterston, Alisse and Maria D. Vesperi, eds. 2009. *Anthropology off the Shelf: Anthropologists on Writing.* New York, NY: Wiley Blackwell.

Waterston, Alisse and Barbara Rylko-Bauer. 2006. "Out of the Shadows of History and Memory: Personal Family Narratives in Ethnographies of Rediscovery." *American Ethnologist*, 33(3): 397–412.

Wulff, Helena, ed. 2016. *The Anthropologist as Writer: Genres and Contexts in the Twenty-First Century.* London: Berghahn Books.

Index

About the Editors

Ida Fadzillah Leggett is an associate professor of Anthropology in the Department of Sociology and Anthropology at Middle Tennessee State University (MTSU). She received her Doctorate in Cultural Anthropology from the University of Illinois, Urbana-Champaign in 2003, for which she conducted field research in Northern Thailand on teenage girls and the effects of education and globalization on their "life strategy narratives." Her research publications include "'Better Childhoods' as Immigration Narrative (Not) Told Through Food," in *Global Studies of Childhood* and "Negotiating Dangerous Spaces: Encounters with Prostitution and AIDS in Northern Thailand" in *Ruminations on Violence*. She is currently working on a research project on girl culture, imagination, and future aspirations.

William H. Leggett is an associate professor of Anthropology at Middle Tennessee State University. He has worked on issues of globalization and post-colonialism in Southeast Asia. His publications include the book *The Flexible Imagination: at work in the transnational corporate offices of Jakarta, Indonesia*, and the articles "Instituting the Colonial Imagination: Chinese middlemen and the transnational corporate office in Jakarta, Indonesia," and "Terror and the Colonial Imagination at work in the corporate offices of Jakarta, Indonesia."

About the Contributors

Denielle Elliott is a sociocultural anthropologist at York University where she is the deputy director of the Tubman Institute. Her research explores the (1) anthropology of state science and scientists; (2) settler colonialism/ urban Indigeneity; (3) the anthropology of biosciences; and (4) multimodal ethnographic methods. She is currently working on two projects: an arts-based ethnography of traumatic brain injuries and a second project that explores the history of Canadian microbiology research on infectious diseases. She is a founding member of the Centre for Imaginative Ethnography, and coeditor of *A Different Kind of Ethnography* (2016). She is also the author of *Reimagining Science and Statecraft in Postcolonial Kenya: Stories from an African Scientist* (2018). She has published papers in Cultural Studies Review, Anthropology and Humanism, Catalyst, Medicine Anthropology Theory, among other journals and edited books.

Angela Glaros is associate professor of Anthropology and Women's, Gender, and Sexuality Studies at Eastern Illinois University. She received her doctorate from the University of Illinois at Urbana-Champaign in 2011. Her dissertation examined gender and traditional vocal music on the Greek island of Skyros. Since 2013, she has been involved in ethnographic research on the power of women's voices in Greek Orthodox Christian liturgical music in East Central Illinois.

Daniel Mains is associate professor of Anthropology and African Studies in the Honors College at the University of Oklahoma. Daniel is the author of *Hope Is Cut: Youth, Unemployment, and the Future in Urban Ethiopia* and *Under Construction: Technologies of Development in Urban Ethiopia*.

He is currently researching the politics of infrastructure and urban growth in Norman, Oklahoma.

Derek Pardue, PhD, is associate professor of Brazilian Studies inside the Global Studies Department at Aarhus University in Denmark. He is a cultural anthropologist, who has focused on issues of migration, urbanism and identity politics throughout the Black Atlantic, specifically the Luso-African world of Brazil, Portugal, and Cape Verde. He recently finished his tenure as a senior fellow at the Hanse-Wissenschaftskolleg Institute in Germany (www.h-w-k.de/en/hwk-overview.html), where he wrote a book of ethnographic fiction featuring newly arrived West African and Haitian migrants in São Paulo, Brazil. Publications include the following: *Cape Verde, Let's Go: Creole Rappers and Citizenship in Portugal* (2015), *Brazilian Hip-Hoppers Speak from the Margin: We's on Tape* (2011) and the edited volumes *Living (Il)legalities in Brazil* (2020) and *Ruminations on Violence* (2008).

Judith Pintar is an associate teaching professor and the acting director of the Undergraduate Program in the School of Information Science at the University of Illinois at Urbana-Champaign. Her recent work centers around collaborative knowledge practices, and game studies. She is a game designer and director of an Illinois campus-wide game studies initiative: Games@ Illinois: Playful Design for Transformative Education." Her broader interests include suggestibility and media manipulation, and trauma and memory studies. She has a master's degree in Anthropology and PhD in Sociology, from the University of Illinois at Urbana-Champaign.

9 781793 643988